How Long Can the Moon Be Caged?

'A telling account of repression and resistance in the new India.'
—Jean Drèze, Indian economist

'A brave and necessary record of how, behind tall prison walls, some of India's finest hearts and minds are locked away by a state fearful of their dreams. A book of aching, terrible beauty, bearing witness to the stubborn endurance of idealism, of courage and humanity shining through soul-numbing injustice.'
—Harsh Mander, writer, human rights and peace worker, teacher

'Those who want to understand the nature of today's political regime in India need to read this book. Focusing on the situation of dozens of political prisoners whose words had never been reproduced so extensively so far, it shows how the Modi government is criminalising dissent. The demise of the rule of law is precipitated by the instrumentalisation of the security apparatus and the making of a "parallel regime of truth".'
—Christophe Jaffrelot, Professor of Indian Politics and Sociology, King's College London

'An important testament to the dystopian state of the nation through powerful documentation of the incarceration of dissent in contemporary India.'
—Alpa Shah, author of *Nightmarch: Among India's Revolutionary Guerrillas*

How Long Can the Moon Be Caged?

Voices of Indian Political Prisoners

Suchitra Vijayan and Francesca Recchia

PLUTO  PRESS

First published 2023 by Pluto Press
New Wing, Somerset House, Strand, London WC2R 1LA
and Pluto Press, Inc.
1930 Village Center Circle, 3-834, Las Vegas, NV 89134

www.plutobooks.com

British Library Cataloguing in Publication Data
A catalogue record for this book is available from the British Library

ISBN 978 0 7453 4798 1   Paperback
ISBN 978 0 7453 4800 1   PDF
ISBN 978 0 7453 4799 8   EPUB
ISBN 978 0 7453 4928 2   Audio

This book is printed on paper suitable for recycling and made from fully managed and sustained forest sources. Logging, pulping and manufacturing processes are expected to conform to the environmental standards of the country of origin.

Typeset by Stanford DTP Services, Northampton, England
Simultaneously printed in the United Kingdom and United States of America

To all those who fight for freedom

Contents

Introduction

At no time have governments been moralists.
They never imprisoned people and executed them for having
   done something.
They imprisoned and executed them to keep them from doing
   something.

– Aleksandr Solzhenitsyn, The Gulag Archipelago, 1918–56

In March 2020, at The Polis Project we launched the publication of a series called 'Profiles of Dissent', centring remarkable voices of courage and their histories. The focus of the series was on political prisoners in India. The idea started from a collaboration with maraa, a Bangalore-based media and arts collective who had put together a self-published pamphlet titled *Read Aloud. Ideas Can Never Be Arrested* (2019), where they gave an update on the status of the cases of the so-called BK16 along with a selection of their writings. As often happens at The Polis Project, the 'Profiles' soon took a life of their own, people started sending requests to write and include new stories and it became a collective initiative with the publication of 27 profiles to date from India, Kashmir and Pakistan. 'Profiles of Dissent' turned out to be an occasion to think about the ways in which state violence and judicial complicity can fundamentally remake societies.

In Indian and international media, BK16 has become the shorthand for the 16 individuals who have been implicated for abetting the violence that broke out in the Bhima Koregaon village in the state of Maharashtra on 1 January 2018 between Dalit activists and right-wing militants. They were then successively accused of being part of a conspiracy to kill the Indian Prime Minister Narendra Modi. The BK16 are Sudha Bharadwaj, Arun Ferreira, Surendra Gadling, Mahesh Raut, Shoma Sen, Rona Wilson, Sudhir Dhawale, Vernon Gonsalves, Varavara Rao, Gautam Navlakha, Anand Teltumbde, Hany Babu, Stan Swamy, Sagar Gorkhe, Ramesh Gaichor and Jyoti Jagtap. These people are artists, lawyers, poets, activists, public intellectuals and human rights defenders; some of them were personally connected, most knew about each other because of the relevance of their work, some only met each other in person for the first time in court during the hearings of the case.

In March 2020, sub-inspector Arvind Kumar of the Delhi Crime Branch filed the infamous First Information Report (FIR) 59 claiming that there was a conspiracy whereby the February 2020 Delhi pogrom was planned by people who used the anti-Citizenship Amendment Act (CAA) protests to mobilise the masses against the government. On 18 February 2020, ruling Bharatiya Janata Party (BJP) politician Kapil Mishra had declared in front of a crowd that he and his supporters would be 'forced to hit the streets' if the police would not clear the sites of the anti-CAA protests. This incendiary speech triggered mass violence across predominantly Muslim Northeast Delhi that raged on for four days. Multiple tes-timonies, corroborated by independent investigations, have shown that the fury of right-wing mobs was uncontrollable and that police forces stood by and did nothing to restrain them. As a result of the pogrom, 53 people were murdered, the majority of them Muslim, and hundreds of Muslim families lost homes and property and, at the time of writing, are still displaced.[1]

Following these events, Kapil Mishra walked away untouched and Arvind Kumar filed the FIR 59 against 19 people, mostly Muslim community leaders and student activists: Faizan Khan, Sharjeel Imam, Umar Khalid, Natasha Narwal, Devangana Kalita, Ishrat Jahan, Gulfisha Fatima, Meeran Haider, Safoora Zargar, Asif Iqbal Tanha, Taahir Hussain, Mohd Parvez Ahmed, Mohd Illyas, Khalid Saifi, Shahdab Ahmed, Tasleem Ahmed, Saleem Malik, Mohd Saleem Khan and Athar Khan. The accusations against them

---

1.   The Polis Project. 'The high cost of targeted violence in Northeast Delhi: a list of the deceased.' *The Polis Project*, 2 March 2020; Youth for Human Rights Documentation, 'An account of fear and impunity – a preliminary fact finding report on communally-targeted violence in NE Delhi, February 2020.' *The Polis Project*, 8 March 2020. The Polis Project was the first organisation to argue for the definition of the events as a pogrom rather than riots or generic violence given the blatant connivance and complicity between police forces and the perpetrators of the violence against members of the Muslim minority community.

are based on the revelations made to the police sub-inspector by an anonymous informer, who claimed to know that Jawaharlal Nehru University (JNU) student Umar Khalid was hatching a conspiracy to cause communal violence and that the upheaval intentionally coincided with US President Donald Trump's visit to India to discredit the image of the government in front of the world.[2]

Fast forward to June 2022: Nupur Sharma and Naveen Jindal – respectively, the former BJP spokesperson and the former head of the Delhi BJP's media unit – made derogatory remarks about Prophet Mohammad that triggered a massive wave of protests across the country with thousands of Muslims taking to the streets. A week after the incident, the police in the state of Uttar Pradesh (UP) – one of the main epicentres of the agitation – reported to have arrested 415 people and to have registered 20 FIRs in connection to the violence. In yet another conspiracy case, activist and Welfare Party leader Javed Mohammad was named as one of the 'key conspirators' in the protests, arrested and later charged also under the National Security Act, 1980 (NSA), which allows for up to a year of detention without charge or trial. It is worth noting that Javed Mohammad did not take part in any of the protests.

These three events represent key moments in the recent history of India, in which the state has moved with all its might to silence and criminalise dissent. In none of these instances, however, have the actual perpetrators been prosecuted or convicted whereas in all of them, the state, the police, the judiciary and the media have worked together to fabricate and amplify the hatching of conspiracies.

We saw this pattern emerge over and over again: the police, with the tacit approval of the judiciary, let the perpetrators of heinous acts of violence and hate speech walk away while targeting individuals or entire communities affected by the violence as criminals. Key witnesses died in mysterious ways and manufactured evidence was used as the basis to arrest people. The media, in all these instances, played a crucial role in justifying the state's version of the story.

---

2. Umar Khalid's appeal for bail was dismissed by the Delhi High Court on 18 October 2022 stating that the allegations against Khalid were prima facie true.

Conspiracies are by their very nature murky businesses: they are secretive, whispered and, ultimately, hard to prove. As Narendra Modi grows more hieratic in tone, vision and appearance so is the language of conspiracy growing wilder and more widespread in his management of political opponents. Both trends bank exclusively on faith and belief so much so that, spun by an incredibly powerful propaganda machine, they make for the perfect recipe for success in the current post-truth regime. This deadly combination, on the one hand, nurtures an atmosphere of tension and a climate of constant suspicion if not utter terror; on the other, it gives a freehand to Modi's followers who perpetrate violence in order to defend their leader and his ideology by any means possible. This is how vigilante squads, lynching and communal violence have become the norm and how those who dare to contest the status quo are indicted as criminals and treated with unrestrained cruelty and brutality.

Facts and evidence have thus become accessories for a state that manufactures its enemies. This kind of fabrication, however, does not happen overnight nor does it happen in a vacuum: it needs planning, obedience and complicity as well as money for its stealth implementation. Combing operations, 'bulldozer justice',[3] the use and misuse of laws and regulations, internet trolls and cyber surveillance are all activities that require complex logistics and vast concerted efforts. They need a complacent judiciary, complicit army and police forces, obedient local authorities and subservient media.

The latest development in the case against Professor G.N. Saibaba is an egregious example of this entanglement of connivances and of

---

3. This expression started to be frequently used after Ajay Mohan Singh Bisht, or Yogi Adityanath, a right-wing Hindu monk, became the chief minister of Uttar Pradesh in 2017. Since he took office, his government has used demolitions as a political tool to target various Muslim communities in the state. The term implies the extrajudicial and illegal use of bulldozers to target and demolish predominantly Muslim homes, businesses, shrines, graves and places of worship, including a sixteenth-century mosque, without due process, leading to mass forced displacement. Demolitions are punitive and are now used systematically to manufacture dispossession across multiple states, including Madhya Pradesh, Rajasthan, Karnataka, Uttarakhand as well as Delhi's Jahangirpuri area.

how even the Supreme Court of India is part of this machination. In October 2022, the Court convened a special two-judges bench early on a Saturday morning to suspend the acquittal of Saibaba and five others and stay their release order that was issued by the Bombay High Court less than 24 hours earlier.[4] We will examine the persecution of Professor G.N. Saibaba in detail in the next chapters, but here it is worth noting that Justice M.R. Shah – one of the two members of the bench – went on record with this oral remark during the hearing: 'So far as terrorist or Maoist activities are concerned, the brain is more dangerous. Direct involvement is not necessary.'

Pandu Narote, an Adivasi from Gadchiroli district in Maharashtra, was convicted along with Saibaba under various terror laws in 2017 and died in custody at the age of 33 after contracting swine flu in August 2022. In a telephone conversation, Narote's lawyer Akash Sorde told us that the family was not informed about his deteriorating health. Instead, they were kept in the dark and 'only found out through the news'.

Sorde believes that Narote was denied medical treatment until his condition deteriorated severely. 'There was blood in his vomit and urine. They waited till the last minute when he was already on his deathbed to shift him to the hospital. It was too late.' Sorde said that Narote's wife and daughter had not seen him since his conviction in 2017: 'The family lives deep in the forest and never had the resources to visit him.' Saibaba's lawyer Nihalsing Rathod said that Narote's death, in its own right, implies that the institutional murder of G.N. Saibaba is a virtual certainty.[5]

After Father Stan Swamy and Kanchan Nanaware, Pandu Narote is one more political prisoner to die after being deliberately denied medical treatment and taken to hospital when he was close to death.

---

4. Sohini Chowdhury, 'Supreme Court stays release of Prof G.N. Saibaba & others in UAPA case, suspends Bombay HC's acquittal order.' *LiveLaw.in*, 15 October 2022.
5. Harsh Thakor, 'Pandu Narote's death is a perfect illustration of neo-fascist murder by the state.' *Countercurrents*, 27 August 2022.

How did this moment come to be? For this we need to go back in time to understand how India's national security was built over a decade and transformed into a well-oiled machine of oppression.

A week after G.N. Saibaba was abducted from his home, a newly elected BJP government under Prime Minister Modi stormed into power in May 2014.

During his years as chief minister of Gujarat (2001–14), the state became the laboratory of the Hindutva experiment – an exclusionary, autocratic ethno-nationalist idea of a Hindu India. Under his rule, Gujarat's Muslim population saw indiscriminate state and extrajudicial violence, targeted killings and political assassinations following the 2002 pogrom. Yet, in all these cases, Modi was given a clean chit by the Supreme Court of India, stating that there was 'no prosecutable evidence'.

Most of those who resisted were either jailed or dead.[6]

Modi's much hyped growth and development Gujarat Model was in reality an aggressive implementation of development on behalf of big private investors: working for the rich and against the poor. It was an explosive mix of policies and actions that enabled violent Hindu nationalism and crony capitalism to flourish. Before becoming prime minister, during his electoral campaign, Modi repeatedly defined himself as a 'muscular nationalist' and regularly used hate speech in his rallies. Then, with his landslide win in 2014, he used the Gujarat Model of authoritarian populism to run the country.

Immediately after his elections, Modi aggressively pushed the Make in India campaign and lobbied for unmitigated 'development' in Adivasi areas criminalising anyone who opposed it. Development became the facade for legalised plunder. While the Indian state has a long brutal history of deploying state violence to reach its goal, with Modi what previous governments did in the blanket of the night – in the realm of the extrajudicial, the covert and the illegal – quickly became the norm.

---

6.   The Wire Staff, 'IPS officer who questioned Modi's role in Gujarat riots gets life in 30-year-old case.' *The Wire*, 20 June 2019; Outlook Web Desk, 'A midnight meeting on Feb 27 and a murdered minister.' *Outlook India*, 12 November 2007.

Modi's regime ushered in a new era of autocracy – where all authority was vested in the prime minister's office with hardly any checks on his power. As a result, since Modi came to power there has been a rapid disintegration of institutions and a decline of civil liberties along with the consolidation of a security state that disregards questions of privacy, human rights and personal freedoms.

Almost all institutions – the judiciary, the police, civil society and the media – have been systematically defanged or stacked with ideological foot soldiers of the regime. Each of these institutions, in turn, now dutifully fulfil its role in defending the regime's policies, propaganda and violence, while simultaneously criminalising dissent and targeting anyone who challenged the government's policies. Critical and dissenting voices have become anti-nationals, Urban Naxals, Maoists or *Tukde Tukde* gang.[7]

The police and the National Investigation Agency (NIA) started using counter-insurgency tactics against civil society – writers, lawyers, activists, community leaders, students and almost anyone who spoke against the government. It began with scholars and human rights activists like Saibaba and Binayak Sen, who worked to support Adivasi communities in Maoist strongholds. It quickly turned into a wider attack on critical intellectuals, journalists and students in academic spaces. Some were arrested, others were killed – social activist Narendra Dabholkar in 2013; scholar M.M. Kalburgi in 2015; followed by Gauri Lankesh, editor of a Kannada language weekly and a journalist turned activist, who was shot in 2017; and Communist politician Govind Pansare in 2018. Investigations showed interconnections between all these assassinations and that the accused are related to the Sanatan Sanstha and the

---

7.   The terms 'anti-nationals', 'Urban Naxals', 'Maoists' and *Tukde Tukde* (Breaks India) gang are used to describe individuals, groups and members of civil society who are labelled as a threat to national security. The usage of the terms is highly controversial and politically charged. 'Naxal' is used to refer to a member or supporter of the Naxalite movement, a left-wing extremist group that originated in the late 1960s. They have been involved in a long-standing insurgency in various parts of India, particularly in rural areas where they mobilise peasants and workers against state and capitalist interests. 'Urban Naxals' broadly refers to progressive urban intelligentsia. *Tukde Tukde* gang refers to individuals or groups supposedly working to break up the unity and integrity of India by promoting separatist movements in different regions of the country.

Hindu Janjagruti Samiti, both radical Hindutva organisations implicated in these murders.[8]

In India, national security is the holy cow, in whose name almost any egregious violation of fundamental rights is now possible. However, the current architecture of terror laws did not emerge in a vacuum. In the immediate aftermath of 9/11, the then Indian BJP prime minister, Atal Bihari Vajpayee, gave a rousing speech: 'Every Indian has to be a part of this global war on terrorism. We must, and we will, stamp out this evil from our land and from the world. Jai Hind!'[9]

Soon after, the Prevention of Terrorism Act (POTA) came into force in October 2001 as a presidential ordinance modelled after the American Patriot Act. Under this law, people could be arrested solely based on suspicion and detained without charge or trial for six months.[10] POTA further expanded police powers and allowed for special investigations, courts and trial procedures. POTA was in use from 2001 to 2004 and the law's victims were disproportionately Muslim.[11] While the extrajudicial powers granted through POTA were repealed in 2004, many oppressive measures were legislated into the criminal code through amendments to the Unlawful Activities Prevention Act (UAPA) of 2004.

The 2008 Mumbai terror attacks bequeathed the new national security state with more power and almost no restraint. By the end of the year, the NIA, a new counter-terrorist task force, was established to deal with terror-related activities in India and the draconian UAPA was amended again. The amended UAPA laws gave the police the ability to search, seize and arrest any person

8. T.A. Johnson, 'Explained: Dabholkar-Lankesh murders – what the investigations into violent right-wing activism show.' *The Indian Express*, 26 May 2019; Deborah Grey, 'Death of a rationalist: Gauri Lankesh.' *CJP*, 13 May 2018.

9. Cited in Reece Jones, 'Geopolitical boundary narratives, the global war on terror and border fencing in India.' *Transactions of the Institute of British Geographers*, 34, 2009: 290–304.

10. Around 3,500 people in 18 Indian states (including a few children in Jharkhand and Tamil Nadu) were held under POTA for varying periods. Gujarat had the highest number of detentions and all but one of the 287 people initially held under the act were Muslims.

11. Anil Kalhan et al., 'Colonial continuities: human rights, terrorism, and security laws in India.' *Columbia Journal of Asian Law*, 2006, p. 93.

without a warrant and detain any person for 30 days in police custody and 180 days in judicial custody without a chargesheet.

For the first time, these laws made preventive detention the norm and bail the exception.

Unlike the UAPA, previous terror laws like TADA (Terrorist and Disruptive Activities Prevention Act, 1987) and POTA had a sunset clause. Under the sunset provision, terror laws were reviewed for renewal every two years. Doing away with sunset clauses essentially inscribed emergency powers into the legal system.

The funds allocated to the various intelligence agencies increased along with their unlimited powers. In 2016, the Supreme Court refused to admit a Public Interest Litigation (PIL) that 'sought greater scrutiny of the funds and actions of the country's key intelligence agencies, including the Intelligence Bureau, Research and Analysis Wing and National Technical Research Organisation'.[12] The PIL stated: 'India is the only democracy in the world whose intelligence agencies are not accountable to the Parliament or people.'

Since 2016, the Government of India has again increased the budget of the Intelligence Bureau, the country's domestic intelligence, internal security and counter-intelligence agency by a further 16 percent.[13] The NIA, with unfettered powers, has become the repressive tool used to crush all forms of dissent. The Bhima Koregaon conspiracy case, the Delhi violence case and the numerous arrests of journalists are built almost entirely based on UAPA provisions, with the NIA leading the charge.

After Modi returned to power in 2019, the UAPA was amended again and gave authorities the power to unilaterally designate anyone as a terrorist without evidence, reversing the burden of proof. The accused now have to prove their innocence as against the state having to prove their guilt. The amendment did not define who a terrorist is and gave the NIA power to investigate terror cases giving primacy to the 'interests of India' – the language is intentionally vague and does not define what (or whose) these interests

---

12.   Samanwaya Rautray, 'Greater scrutiny of RAW & IB will risk own existence: Supreme Court.' *The Economic Times*, 14 July 2018.
13.   Ibid.

are. The vagueness of the language quickly remade writers, thinkers, artists, activists, students and union leaders into terrorists.

The amendment also transferred police powers currently under the local state government to the NIA and other central agencies. Human trafficking, counterfeit currency-related offences and cyber-terrorism offences were previously under state policing powers; this shift of control makes the union government all-powerful while eroding the states' jurisdictions. In a 1977 Supreme Court judgment, Justice V.R. Krishna Iyer stated: 'The basic rule may perhaps be tersely put as bail, not jail.'[14] The UAPA has reversed this dictum to 'jail, not bail'.

The UAPA is used to detain people indefinitely without trial. It is not meant to fight terrorism or adjudicate the charges. Most of the UAPA cases end up in acquittals. A People's Union for Civil Liberties' (PUCL) study found that 97.2 percent of those held under the UAPA for long periods were eventually acquitted.[15] Of the 8,371 persons arrested under the UAPA between 2015 and 2020, only 235 were convicted.[16]

These are some of the many examples that demonstrate how the current Indian dispensation is incredibly effective and efficient in joining forces to create an airtight system of criminalisation of dissent. As a result, anyone who comes in the way of the implementation of the Hindu Rashtra is silenced or eliminated. This is why we think it is particularly important to analyse and dissect the status of contemporary authoritarian India starting from the experience of political prisoners.

In some research and activist anti-caste circles in India, there is a growing insistence to consider every prisoner as a political prisoner based on a structural discontent with the carceral system. The arguments, that have parallels with Black American institutional critique, highlight the ingrained injustice of the system as a colonial inheritance of the British Raj and reflect on the disproportionate targeting of individuals (particularly men) who belong to

---

14. State of Rajasthan, Jaipur vs Balchand, 20 September 1977.
15. V. Suresh, S.B. Madhura and Lekshmi Sujatha, 'UAPA: criminalising dissent and state terror.' *PUCL*, 28 September 2022.
16. Ibid.

lower castes, religious and other minorities. Lawyer Disha Wadekar, who represented Dalit survivors before the judicial enquiry commission set up to investigate the caste violence in Bhima Koregaon, opposes individualised definitions of political prisoner. She argues that in the context of India caste privilege shapes also the access to civil liberties and hence to the right to dissent.

Even though it lacks a standard legal definition, the question of political prisoners is unique both at an analytical and at a political level. It is a category of criminal offence that questions the very essence of any societies that call themselves liberal democracies. Political prisoners challenge existing relations of power, question the status quo, confront authoritarianism and injustice; they stand with the disenfranchised. Theirs is a thought crime: the crime of thinking, acting, speaking, probing, reporting, questioning, demanding rights, defending their homes and, ultimately, exercising citizenship. These kinds of arrests and inhumane incarcerations do not just target private acts of courage, they are bound together with questions of citizenship and with people's capacity to hold the state accountable – particularly those states that are unilaterally remaking their relationship with their people. The assault on fundamental rights has been consistent at a global level and rights-bearing citizens have been transformed into consuming subjects of a surveillance state.

India is the torchbearer of this ongoing assault.

In this dystopian landscape, therefore, dissent is sedition and resistance is treason.

A fearful and weak state silences the voice of dissent. Once it has established repression as a response to critique, it has only one way to go: to become a regime of authoritarian terror and the source of dread for its citizens. As fear spreads, criticism retreats from the public domain. For this arbitrary management of law and order, civil society lays low, chooses silence and tries to regroup for the sake of self-preservation.

Rupali Jadhav is one of the members of Kabir Kala Manch (KKM), a working-class Dalit cultural organisation that was set up in Pune after the 2002 Gujarat pogrom. They work with protest songs, poetry and street theatre to promote anti-caste and pro-democracy ideas. They perform songs about caste, gender, agrarian crisis, fascism, imperialism, class struggle and patriarchy. Streets, alleyways, bus stops and slums are their stage, where they combine folk tradition, dance and songs about oppression, caste violence, Brahmanical hegemony and neoliberal plunder. Three KKM members are among the BK16 co-accused: Sagar Gorkhe, Ramesh Gaichor and Jyoti Jagtap. Rupali Jadhav recalls the days in which they were arrested in a cold, almost detached way. They cannot afford to be emotive about it, she told us, and the arrests did not come as a shock: they knew from the very start that, given the existing climate of tyranny, they would end up paying a price for the work they do. For them, as for many other activists, journalists, intellectuals, trade unionists and community leaders, the question is not 'if' they are going to be caught, it is only just 'when'.

Jadhav is adamant about the fact that the Indian state acts following a deliberate and well-oiled strategy of repression and that the targeting of individual voices of dissent is a way to break 'physically, mentally and economically' the communities around them. The arrest of the three KKM members made everyone else in the collective unemployable. Requests for them to perform have drastically reduced as people are scared and have no energy left to deal with the vindictive and unpredictable actions of the state.

In this bracing for the worst to come, there is a constant oscillation between the need to speak up and the necessity to survive. Many former political prisoners acknowledge the numerous acts of generosity they received through their tribulations, but they are also deeply concerned about the fact that this slow but unstoppable persecution of dissent will end up corroding the roots of solidarity.

This erosion of civil society is perhaps the most crucial and least overt aim of the Hindu Rashtra. As the government is on a mission to achieve religious homologation and homogeneity, every expression of otherness should be chased, persecuted, repressed and eventually erased. This is why the 2017 Elgar Parishad meeting triggered their most evil of pulsions and hence the harshest of responses.

Convened on 31 December 2017 in Pune by retired judges P.B. Sawant and B.G. Kolse-Patil – in collaboration with KKM and writer and activist Sudhir Dhawale – the Elgar Parishad was a meeting of around 260 organisations representing diverse sections of civil society across caste, class and religion. The assembly called for a unified fight against growing right-wing Hindu nationalism and gathered in defence of the Indian Constitution. The reign of terror inflicted by Hindutva politics was called the 'New Peshwai'.[17]

Over 35,000 people attended and concluded the event with an unprecedented collective 'oath of allegiance' to stand together and counter the disregard for the Indian Constitution. The participants of the Elgar Parishad pledged 'that we will protect the Constitution and democracy. ... We will not support those who speak against the Constitution or oppose the Constitution. We will never vote for opponents of the Constitution, the RSS (Rashtriya Swayamsevak Sangh), and BJP'.[18]

The following day, many of those who were present at the Elgar Parishad, along with thousands of Dalits, met again in the nearby village of Bhima Koregaon to commemorate the 200th anniversary of the battle of Koregaon, where 49 Dalits were killed fighting against the Peshwai – the dominant caste group that used to rule the region.

Violence broke out in Bhima Koregaon between Hindutva groups and the Dalit community gathered for the commemoration, with the former blaming Dalits claiming they pronounced incendiary speeches during the event. A fact-finding committee appointed by the police, however, found out that the violence was perpetrated by Hindutva mobs and it was fully 'pre-planned'.

Two FIRs were filed based on the competing narratives. As a result, the Hindutva leaders identified as the abettors and instigators of the violence walked away unscathed, while hundreds of Dalits were picked up in combing operations across Maharashtra and the BK16 began their inhuman odyssey.

---

17. The reference is to the dominant caste Peshwai who were part of the Maratha Confederacy ruling the region around Pune. They were defeated on 1 January 1818 in the Battle of Koregaon by troops of the East India Company's Bombay Presidency Army that included a large number of Mahars – or original inhabitants of Maharashtra and one of Dalit (ex-untouchable) caste communities – later followed in great numbers B.R. Ambedkar, who was a Mahar himself and initiated the commemoration. Since then, every 1 January, Dalit communities gather at Bhima Koregaon to celebrate the victory against the Peshwai, whom they see as their oppressors.

18. Shruti Menon and Sreenivasan Jain, 'Videos of Bhima-Koregaon speeches offer a rebuttal to "Maoist" claim.' *NDTV*, 4 September 2018.

From the perspective of a sectarian and ethno-nationalist government, nothing could have been more threatening and despicable than a transversal political allegiance to oppose the status quo and defend the values of the Constitution. It is for this that the state went out of its way to make the BK16 a monumental example of its determination to eliminate any opponents. For this show of strength, the state did not leave any stone unturned: from planting evidence to using the process as the persecution, from denying medical care to remaining unperturbed when undertrials died in custody.[19]

Political prisoners have therefore been turned into the enemy number one: anti-nationals, seditious, traitors, terrorists. Dehumanised through language and punishment, they have been made to embody all that is evil and threatening for the preservation of a homogeneous idea of a Hindu India.

By a specular logic and therefore for the opposite reasons, these political prisoners have become icons of resistance and solidarity in the eyes of all those who consider with dread and fear India's descent to fascist authoritarianism. That is why at the centre of the book are the prisoners themselves and their families of blood or election, the people with whom they share a deep bond of love and are now dedicating their own lives to the prisoners' liberation. These are spouses, partners, children, colleagues, comrades whose lives have been upended by the cruelty of the state. In the two and a half years of the making of this book, we spent time – online during COVID lockdowns and in person after it became possible – with this diverse community of people learning from their experiences, adjusting our priorities following their suggestions, immersing ourselves in this context, thus trying to grasp the enormity of such an upheaval.

These testimonies are at the core of the book. Along with these conversations, we gathered secondary material through Indian and international English-speaking media, advocacy groups, campaigns and human rights platforms. Our access to sources in other Indian languages – Hindi, Urdu, Malayalam and Marathi – was

___

19. Siddhartha Deb, 'The unravelling of a conspiracy: were the 16 charged with plotting to kill India's prime minister framed?' *The Guardian*, 12 August 2021.

made possible by the help of our researchers; the knowledge of these sources is, however, by no means exhaustive.

The work done over the years on state violence at The Polis Project, both with 'Profiles of Dissent' and at Watch The State, proved an important foundation for reflections that have been with us for a long time and now have the chance to fully breathe in the form of a book. While there is no formal literature review to accompany the book, our individual and collective academic research interests have directly or indirectly converged to shape it.

For a deliberate political and methodological choice, we decided not to include in the book stories of political prisoners from Kashmir and the Indian North East. Indian occupied Kashmir is an egregious example of settler colonialism and, as such, is ruled following the specific diktats of a military occupation. In the North East, struggles for citizenship are preceded by a deeper question of national belonging and the relentless application of the Armed Forces Special Powers Act (AFSPA, 1990) creates an absolute lack of accountability. Both of these contexts require a specific political analysis and a separate set of parameters and observations rather than being grouped under rubrics that are valid in mainland India: both Kashmir and the North East would in fact deserve separate books on the situation of their political prisoners. Their absence is therefore not an oversight, but an acknowledgement of their uniqueness and specificity: it is for this reason that we do not want to create false equivalences and similes.

How Long Can the Moon Be Caged? takes its title from the line quoted in a letter that Natasha Narwal sent from jail and it is constructed as a reversed pyramid. We start with a broad picture and then move on to a very tight close up: from a contextual analysis of the current political situation in India, we zoom in on the experience of political prisoners from their own perspective and through their own voices.

In this introduction we tried to make sense of what it means, politically, to look at the present through the engagement with the struggle for the freedom of political prisoners. While some critics believe that every prisoner is a political prisoner, in this book we insist on the urgency of the specificity of such a notion given the set of preconditions (and persecutions) that are necessary for their very existence.

In the chapter 'A Season of Arrests' we construct a timeline, a calendarisation of the daily efforts that the Modi government put in place in the systematic criminalisation of dissent. Events put in a linear sequence show how the relentlessness in the persecution of political opponents is only possible if all state agencies are actively and obediently participating in the implementation of such a complex plan. The construction and consolidation of the Hindu Rashtra is only possible if everyone works towards it: from the street mob to the highest authorities in the judiciary. The timeline shows how this collaboration took shape day after day, month after month, resulting in scores of politically motivated arrests, police violence and collective punishments.

In the chapter 'Wages of Impunity: Cracking Down on Dissent' we tell the story of democracy receding, rights withering and making way to a profoundly authoritarian state that is intolerant of dissent. We map illegal searches, arrests, abductions, disappearances, judicial decisions and misdemeanours by police officers and analyse how these events have corroded fundamental constitutional values over time. We articulate how the Indian prison system and the courts have become complicit in denying people their basic rights. The chapter opens with the illegal abduction of G.N. Saibaba and the incarceration of Binayak Sen and culminates in the arrests of BK16 and of Muslim students and activists after the 2020 Delhi pogrom. What emerges is a frightening story of state impunity and criminalisation of dissent.

In 'The Lies Factory', we look at the ways in which the Indian government manipulates words to create parallel regimes of truth that ignore facts so as to serve its own political aims. We highlight in particular how the judiciary and the Supreme Court have been blindly following political demands and, under such pressure, have rather been keeping people in jail than standing up for evidence and justice.

As we begin to narrow the focus, 'A Community in Resistance' is a chapter that reconstructs in an intimate tone the pains and hopes of the community that gravitates around the political prisoners and their families. The narrative is the result of firsthand testimonies collected over time in meetings, conversations and interviews. What emerges is a portrait of dignity and rectitude, which is incredibly more complex and nuanced than trite arguments of victimisation and oppression: there is sorrow and fatigue, there is despair and incomprehension, but there is also a very deep sense of purpose that is nurtured by love, by the quest for justice and by the spirit of resistance.

'Small Things' is the outcome of the close collaboration with the families of the political prisoners. Before being admitted to jail, people are asked to leave behind all the things they carry, all the objects that in some way contribute to make them who they are. It is just one of the many efforts to dehumanise them. That is why we asked families if there was an object or a 'thing' that they would immediately associate with their loved ones who are in jail. We also asked the former political prisoners if there was a 'thing' they connected to their experience in jail. The result is a collection of photos – taken by the families or the former prisoners themselves – that offers an incredibly moving and intimate glimpse in the lives of those who fight for political freedom.

In 'Voices of Indian Political Prisoners' we put together a selection of mostly unpublished material written by political prisoners while in jail. Presented in chronological order, it is a diverse selection of short stories, poems, journal entries, fragments, letters – it is as diverse as the prisoners themselves who are unique and remarkable individuals. Political prisoners are very often spoken about even though they are in jail for their own ideas – this section of the book aims to make a little space to listen to their voice and their thoughts that, however much behind bars, are certainly not incarcerated.

We conclude the book with 'Name the Names', a list of all the Indian political prisoners who have been targeted by the Indian state under the Modi government. We state their name, the charges under which they have been incarcerated, the number of days they spent in jail and the current status of their case. The list was last updated on 10 March 2023 and it is sadly impossible to claim it as complete since the Indian state is relentless in its ongoing persecution and criminalisation of dissent. This list is meant to be a resource, a record of public memory and a way to pay respect to every single individual who is persecuted for their ideas beyond the anonymity of statistics.

As *How Long Can the Moon Be Caged?* is very much the product of its times, we felt the need to close the book on a personal note with an epilogue titled 'When the State Enters Your Home.' Afreen Fatima's home was bulldozed by the Indian state in June 2022, she was working with us on this book and a significant amount of material she had collected for it was destroyed along with the house. Even though we are not particularly in the habit of talking about ourselves, we thought it was important to make an exception and share what this direct confrontation with Indian state violence meant for us and for this book.

1

A Season of Arrests

Even though Indian state agencies have been complicit in curbing dissent for decades, things have dramatically changed with the coming to power of Narendra Modi as prime minister in 2014. His leadership marks an escalation of state violence and impunity where everyone – from street mobs to the courts – works tacitly in support of the Hindu Rashtra. Starting the timeline with key events that took place since Modi's tenure, we show how his ethno-nationalist project has taken shape day after day, month after month, resulting in scores of politically motivated arrests, police violence and collective punishments.

* * *

9 May 2014 – G.N. Saibaba is arrested by Maharashtra's Gadchiroli Police on charges of being associated with the banned Communist Party of India Maoist (CPI Maoist). Saibaba is later suspended by Delhi University.

16 May 2014 – The results of the general elections held between 7 April and 12 May are announced declaring the victory of the BJP with 31 percent of the vote and 282 seats.

26 May 2014 – Narendra Modi, the parliamentary leader of the BJP, is sworn in as the 14th Prime Minister of India.

2 September 2014 – Kanchan Nanaware is arrested along with her husband Arun Bhelke by the Anti Terrorism Squad (ATS) for their alleged links with banned CPI (Maoist).

30 June 2015 – After being lodged in Nagpur Central Jail for 14 months, G.N. Saibaba is granted three months bail for his deteriorating health.

28 September 2015 – In Bisahda village, Dadri, UP a mob of villagers attack 52-year-old Mohammed Akhlaq and lynch him for suspicion of slaughtering a cow.

26 December 2015 – G.N. Saibaba's bail is cancelled and he surrenders before the Central Jail authorities as per the directive of the Nagpur Bench of the Bombay High Court.

4 April 2016 – The Supreme Court grants G.N. Saibaba bail saying that the Maharashtra government has been 'extremely unfair' to him. Saibaba's request of reinstatement as a professor is looked into by a one-member committee constituted by the university's governing body.

26 April 2016 – The Delhi University Teachers Association supports G.N. Saibaba's request of reinstatement, which is opposed by the right-wing Akhil Bharatiya Vidyarthi Parishad (ABVP) – the student wing of the RSS – claiming that the move would have a 'bad influence' on students.

7 March 2017 – G.N. Saibaba and five others are sentenced to life by Gadchiroli Court for criminal conspiracy, criminal activity and for being associated with terrorist organisations.

22 June 2017 – 16-year-old Junaid Khan is stabbed to death and thrown off a running train and four others injured in a religiously motivated attack.

28 December 2017 – The shrine of Vudhu Budhruk village near Bhima Koregaon dedicated to Dalit icon Govind Gaikwad is desecrated. An FIR is filed against the desecrators: groups linked to the RSS, including Milind Ekbote, a well-known Hindutva leader.

31 December 2017 – The Elgar Parishad – a meeting of around 260 organisations representing diverse castes – is held in Pune. Convened by retired judges P.B. Sawant and B.G. Kolse-Patil, the Parishad is called against Hindutva sectarianism and in defence of the Indian Constitution. About 35,000 people attend and the meeting ends with an oath of allegiance to the Indian Constitution.

1 January 2018 – Many of those present at the Elgar Parishad, along with thousands of Dalits, meet in Bhima Koregaon (about 30 kilometres from Pune) to celebrate the 200th anniversary of the battle of Koregaon where 49 Dalits died fighting against the Peshwai, the dominant caste rulers of the region. Violence breaks out between Hindutva groups and the Dalit community gathered in Bhima Koregaon. Hindutva groups claim that violence broke out because of incendiary speeches during the event, but a police-appointed fact-finding committee finds that the violence was 'pre-planned'. Two sets of FIRs are filed based on these competing narratives. The first is filed by Anita Sawale, an anti-caste activist, against Hindutva leaders Sambhaji Bhide and Milind Ekbote for planning and inciting mobs against Dalits. Ekbote is arrested and released; Bhide is investigated but never arrested. The other FIR is filed by Tushar Damgude, a disciple of Bhide, alleging that violence was instigated by individuals with links to banned Naxalite groups at the Elgar Parishad.

3 January 2018 – Dalit groups organise a peaceful *bandh*. Despite the FIR against Sambhaji Bhide and Milind Ekbote for spreading communal violence, the Pune Police crack down on Dalits: 95 people are charged with attempted murder, over 3,000 people are illegally detained and more than 200 Dalit youth arrested.

20 March 2018 – In relation to the Scheduled Caste and Scheduled Tribe (Prevention of Atrocities) Act, 1989, the Supreme Court rules that no arrests can be made without prior permission and allows a court to grant an anticipatory bail if it finds the complaint prima facie an abuse of the law.

2 April 2018 – Thousands of people from Scheduled Castes and Scheduled Tribes announce a national strike in protest of the 20 March Supreme Court decision on the Scheduled Caste and Scheduled Tribe (Prevention of Atrocities) Act, 1989. Dalit slums and homes are targeted and burned down in retaliation.

22 April 2018 – Maharashtra Police special anti-Naxal unit C-60 claims that an encounter took place in Boriya-Kasnasur forest region of Bhamragarh *tehsil* of Gadchiroli district, resulting in the death of 40 people (20 men and 20 women). A month later, a 44-member fact-finding team release its report terming the encounter fake.

6 June 2018 – Pune Police arrest Surendra Gadling, Sudhir Dhawale, Rona Wilson, Shoma Sen and Mahesh Raut under the UAPA for their alleged participation in the Elgar Parishad, alleged links to the banned CPI (Maoist) party and an alleged assassination plot against the prime minister. They, along with other co-accused, will come to be known as BK16.

28 August 2018 – Maharashtra Police raid the homes of Sudha Bharadwaj, Gautam Navlakha, Arun Ferreira, Vernon Gonsalves and Varavara Rao to arrest them under the UAPA. The homes of Anand Teltumbde and Father Stan Swamy are also raided.

29 August 2018 – Five eminent persons (Romila Thapar, Devaki Jain, Satish Deshpande, Prabhat Pattnaik and Maja Daruwala) file a petition in the Supreme Court complaining about the high-handed action of the Maharashtra Police to curb dissenting voices. They complain that Navlakha, Bharadwaj, Rao, Ferreira and Gonsalves were arrested without any credible evidence against them. On the same day, the Supreme Court, unsatisfied with the case's merits, orders that all five are placed under house arrest until 6 September, which is later extended to 19 September.

2 September 2018 – Two days before the 90 days deadline to file a chargesheet in the UAPA case against Gadling, Dhawale, Wilson, Sen and Raut is to expire, a Special Court grants Pune Police a 90-day extension.

28 September 2018 – In a 2:1 vote, the Supreme Court refuses to interfere with the arrests and extends house arrest for Navlakha, Bharadwaj, Rao, Ferreira and Gonsalves for four more weeks.

24 October 2018 – The Bombay High Court quashes the Pune Special Court order for the extension in filing the UAPA charge-sheet against Gadling, Dhawale, Wilson, Sen and Raut.

27 October 2018 – The Pune Police put Ferreira and Gonsalves in police custody; Maharashtra Police take Bharadwaj into police custody; Bombay High Court gives Navlakha a reprieve until 1 November.

29 October 2018 – The Supreme Court stays Bombay High Court order about Navlakha's reprieve and issues a notice on another plea of the Maharashtra Police challenging the Delhi High Court order quashing his transit remand.

15 November 2018 – A nearly 5,000-page chargesheet is filed by the Pune Police accusing Dhawale, Gadling, Wilson, Raut and Sen of inciting violence in Bhima Koregaon. The document absolves Hindutva leaders Ekbote and Bhide on the charges of rioting, violent attacks on Dalits and causing communal disharmony. The chargesheet is filed nearly five months after their arrest and claims the accused had 'active links' with banned CPI (Maoist) party and had helped organise the Elgar Parishad under the banner of Bhima Koregaon Shaurya Din Prerana Abhiyan. The chargesheet is unclear on who perpetrated the violence and who were the victims.

17 November 2018 – Varavara Rao is taken into judicial custody.

23 November 2018 – Pune Police seek an extension of another 90 days to file supplementary chargesheet against Gadling, Dhawale, Wilson, Sen and Raut.

3 December 2018 – The Supreme Court directs the Maharashtra government to produce the chargesheet in the Bhima Koregaon violence case.

15 December 2018 – The Bombay High Court extends relief from arrest to Navlakha until 16 January 2019 and to Teltumbde until 17 December 2018. Stan Swamy's petition is rejected. The three had filed a joint petition to quash an FIR filed by Pune Police against them.

21 February 2019 – A supplementary chargesheet is filed against those arrested in August and specifically against the Indian Association of People's Lawyers (IAPL) – the organisation that works to defend individuals against accusations of Maoists links and that Gonsalves, Ferreira and Bharadwaj are associated with.

11 April 2019 – Voting for the Indian general election begins and continues in different phases across the country until 19 May.

23 May 2019 – Narendra Modi secures a landslide victory in the general election and on 30 May he takes oath for his second mandate.

8 June 2019 – Journalist Prashant Kanojia is arrested for social media comments on UP Chief Minister Adityanath and later released on bail.

17 June 2019 – 24-year-old Tabrez Ansari is attacked by a Hindu mob in Jharkhand, he is tied to a tree, beaten and forced to chant Hindu religious slogans. He dies four days later.

4 August 2019 – A complete internet shutdown and blockage of all communication technologies, including calling on fixed lines and mobile phones, is imposed on Jammu and Kashmir. This internet shutdown, spanning 213 days, will become the longest running internet shutdown in a democracy and the second longest in the world after Myanmar.

5 August 2019 – Article 370 and Article 35A of the Indian Constitution are revoked ending the Jammu and Kashmir special status and turning Jammu and Kashmir and Ladakh into separate Union Territories. News of the revocation is not immediately available to the local population due to the communication blackout.

9 November 2019 – The Supreme Court orders that the disputed land in Ayodhya, the site of the demolished Babri Masjid, is handed over for the construction of a Hindu temple and orders the government to give five acres of land for the construction of a mosque as replacement for Babri Masjid. Thousands of paramilitary forces and police troops are deployed in Ayodhya ahead of the judgment and on the day of the verdict there is an internet shutdown in several cities of UP and Rajasthan; Section 144 is imposed in UP and a number of major cities; schools and colleges are closed in Jammu and Kashmir, Karnataka, Madhya Pradesh, UP and Delhi.

11 December 2019 – The Indian Parliament passes the Citizenship Amendment Act (CAA), a discriminatory law that prevents access to citizenship to Muslims who seek refuge in India and, alongside the National Population Register (NPR) and National Register of Citizens (NRC), puts Muslims in India at risk of statelessness, detention and deportation.

14 December 2019 – Ishwar Nayak is killed as police fire at an anti-CAA protest in Guwahati, Assam.

15 December 2019 – Delhi Police respond with brutality to anti-CAA protests at the Muslim-majority Jamia Millia Islamia University: more than 200 students are injured and around 100 detained. On the same day, students hold protests outside Aligarh Muslim University in Aligarh, UP. The police forcefully enter the campus damaging properties and attack students injuring at least 80.

19 December 2019 – Three anti-CAA protesters are killed in police firing, two in Mangalore (Abdul Jaleel and Nausheen Kudroli) and one in Lucknow (Mohammed Vakil Ahmad).
20 December 2019 – Five anti-CAA protesters are killed in separate police firing incidents across UP.

December 2019–January 2020 – After a new government comes to power in Maharashtra, coalition leader Sharad Pawar calls for the Bhima Koregaon case to be handed over to a Special Investigation Team. The Maharashtra Home Minister Anil Deshmukh calls on 23 January for a meeting for reinvestigation of the case.

24 January 2020 – One day after the meeting on reinvestigating the Bhima Koregaon events, the case is transferred to the union government-controlled NIA – the reason for the decision is not made public.

28 January 2020 – JNU PhD student Sharjeel Imam is arrested by Jehanabad Police in Bihar; he is also booked in multiple FIRs filed in the North Eastern state of Assam and also in Imphal in Manipur and Itanagar in Arunachal Pradesh.

30 January 2020 – Ram Bhakt Gopal, a young Hindu fundamentalist, opens fire at a protest at Jamia Millia Islamia injuring one student. He is arrested and charged with attempted murder.

18 February 2020 – The UP government informs the Allahabad High Court that 22 people were killed in the protests and 883 arrested in connection with violence during anti-CAA protests on 20 and 21 December 2019.

20 February 2020 – 19-year-old student activist Amulya Leona is arrested and booked under sedition charges for shouting 'Hindustan Zindabad! Pakistan Zindabad!' in a rally in Bengaluru.

23 February 2020 – BJP politician Kapil Mishra issues a public statement declaring that his supporters would be 'forced to hit the streets' if the police do not clear anti-CAA protest sites. As a consequence, communal violence breaks out in Gokulpuri, a neighbourhood in Northeast Delhi. From there, it quickly spreads to several other areas – including Seelapur, Shivpuri and Jafrabad – raging on for four days before the situation is finally brought under control. In all, 53 people are murdered, a majority of them Muslim. Hundreds of families, mostly Muslim, are also displaced from their homes.

26 February 2020 – Advocate and former Congress Party councillor Ishrat Jahan and Khalid Saifi, the co-founder of United Against Hate, are arrested by Delhi Police.

6 March 2020 – Sub-inspector Arvind Kumar of the Delhi Crime Branch files the infamous FIR 59 supplementary chargesheet claiming that there was a conspiracy and the Delhi riots were planned by people who used the anti-CAA protests to mobilise the masses against the government. The accused persons are Faizan Khan, Sharjeel Imam, Umar Khalid, Natasha Narwal, Devangana Kalita, Ishrat Jahan, Gulfisha Fatima, Meeran Haider, Safoora Zargar, Asif Iqbal Tanha, Taahir Hussain, Mohd Parvez Ahmed, Mohd Illyas, Saifi Khalid, Shahdab Ahmed, Tasleem Ahmed, Saleem Malik, Mohd Saleem Khan and Athar Khan. Kumar alleged that one of his informers revealed that the conspiracy to cause communal riots was hatched by former-JNU student Umar Khalid and his friends who are associated with different organisations. Kumar's informer claimed that the riot purposely coincided with the visit of the former US President Donald Trump to generate international propaganda about minorities being tortured in India.

11 March 2020 – An organisation called Group of Intellectuals and Academicians – a group with no known intellectual or academic credentials, but with close links to Hindutva outfits – submits a report suggesting that the Delhi violence is the work of an Urban Naxal-jihadi network.

13 March 2020 – Saleem Malik and Mohd Saleem Khan are arrested by Delhi's Dayalpur Police in connection with Delhi violence and granted bail.

16 March 2020 – Former Aam Aadmi Party councillor Tahir Hussain is arrested by the Delhi Police Crime Branch in connection to Delhi violence. He is booked in seven other FIRs by the Delhi Police; in one complaint relating to money laundering being probed by the Enforcement Directorate and in the FIR 59 conspiracy case on 6 April 2020.

21 March 2020 – Ishrat Jahan and Khalid Saifi are granted bail, but immediately re-arrested in the FIR 59 conspiracy case.

24 March 2020 – The Government of India orders a nationwide lockdown to be enforced within four hours from the announcement as a preventive measure against the COVID-19 pandemic.

1 April 2020 – Meeran Haider, the President of Rashtriya Janata Dal's youth wing and a PhD student at Jamia Millia Islamia, is arrested by the Special Cell in the FIR 59 conspiracy case.

6 April 2020 – Shadab Ahmed is arrested by Dayalpur Police in connection to Delhi violence and later booked by the Gokulpuri Police in another case on 7 November 2020. On the same day, journalist Pawan Choudhary is arrested in Bihar on charges of spreading misinformation about the death of a COVID-19 patient.

7 April 2020 – Damodharan, a cameraman with *Sun News*, is arrested and labelled a 'fake journalist' after he recorded staff at a primary health centre in Tamil Nadu handing out medicines to patients without a doctor's prescription. Damodharan will spend ten days in the police station, where he claims to have been physically assaulted.

9 April 2020 – Gulfisha Fatima is first arrested by Delhi's Jafrabad Police in connection to Delhi violence and then booked in the FIR 59 conspiracy case on 20 May 2020. On the same day, Tasleem Ahmed is arrested in connection to Delhi violence, granted bail on 10 June 2020 and then arrested again in the FIR 59 conspiracy case on 24 June 2020.

10 April 2020 – Safoora Zargar is arrested by Delhi's Jafrabad Police in connection to anti-CAA protests. She is granted bail and immediately re-arrested on 13 April 2020 in the FIR 59 conspiracy case.

14 April 2020 – Anand Teltumbde and Gautam Navlakha surrender to the NIA. In spite of health risks from the global pandemic, the Supreme Court dismisses interim relief from arrest.

15 April 2020 – Mumbai Police arrest journalist Rahul Kulkarni for 'rumour-mongering' after he had reported that an official notice announced that railways may open new trains for migrants stuck in large cities. Railway officials later claimed that the notice was not for public dissemination. Police accuse Kulkarni of violating several sections of the Indian Penal Code (IPC) for which, if charged and convicted, he could face up to three years in prison. He is released on bail the following day.

23 April 2020 – Andrew Sam Raja Pandian, founder of news portal *SimpliCity*, is arrested in Coimbatore in the state of Tamil Nadu for filing reports on shortage of food and safety kits at the Coimbatore Medical College Hospital. The Assistant Commissioner of the Coimbatore Corporation files a complaint calling the report 'false' and 'provocative'. Pandian is accused of violating the Epidemic Diseases Act, 1897 and two sections of the IPC and is granted bail by a local court after executing a bond for Rs. 10,000 (around 120 USD).

26 April 2020 – Shifa Ur Rehman, President of the Alumni Association of Jamia Millia Islamia, is arrested in the FIR 59 conspiracy case.

27 April 2020 – The Andaman and Nicobar Islands Police arrest freelance journalist Zubair Ahmed for a tweet on bizarre local quarantine rules. Ahmed is charged with multiple offences, one of which is non-bailable, and accused of spreading false information and obstructing efforts to contain the spread of COVID. Ahmed is granted bail by a local magistrate on the same day.

11 May 2020 – Dhaval Patel, the editor of the *Face the Nation* news website, is arrested for sedition for an article suggesting that the BJP could replace Vijay Rupani as Gujarat chief minister over mishandling the surge in COVID cases in the state. His lawyer says that Patel was held incommunicado for 72 hours before finally being taken before a judge and charged.

17 May 2020 – Student and activist Asif Iqbal Tanha is first arrested and later booked in the FIR 59 conspiracy case on 19 May 2020.

23 May 2020 – Natasha Narwal and Devangana Kalita, activists with feminist organisation Pinjra Tod, are arrested by Jafrabad Police for anti-CAA protests. Narwal is booked on 26 May 2020 in another case by the New Delhi Crime Branch and in the FIR 59 conspiracy case on 30 May 2020.

24 May 2020 – Reporter Basant Sahu is arrested and later released on bail in Jharkhand for questioning a deputy commissioner about COVID cases and circulating his response. Sahu had asked to confirm if there were any COVID cases in the village of Ichagarh, but the official allegedly denied this and told him to go to bed. Sahu recorded the conversation and circulated it in the news and on social media.

5 June 2020 – The Indian government promulgates three Farm Bills sparking a year-long set of protests, which eventually lead to the revocation of the Bills.

6 June 2020 – Devangana Kalita is booked in the FIR 59 conspiracy case.

10 June 2020 – Amulya Leona is granted default bail.

23 June 2020 – Safoora Zargar, who is 23 weeks pregnant, is granted bail on humanitarian grounds.

25 June 2020 – Saleem Malik and Mohd Saleem Khan are arrested in the FIR 59 conspiracy case.

2 July 2020 – Student Athar Khan is arrested in the FIR 59 conspiracy case.

8 July 2020 – Sharjeel Usmani is arrested after being named in four different FIRs, all filed in December 2019. The key allegation is inciting and participating in the violence that erupted in Aligarh Muslim University campus on 15 December 2019.

28 July 2020 – Professor Hany Babu, the convenor of G.N. Saibaba's defence committee, is arrested in relation to the Bhima Koregaon conspiracy case.

29 July 2020 – Faizan Khan, a mobile phone seller, is arrested in the FIR 59 conspiracy case for having sold a SIM card to co-accused Asif Iqbal Tanha.

18 August 2020 – Prashant Kanojia is arrested again for a retweet that remained online a few minutes but which, according to the police, could disturb communal harmony and hurt religious sentiments. Kanojia is charged with violating no fewer than nine IPC articles, for which the combined maximum sentence is 28 years in prison. Police even accuse him of violating Section 66A of the Information Technology Act, 2000 that was ruled as unconstitutional in 2015.

25 August 2020 – Sharjeel Imam is named in the FIR 59 conspiracy case.

1 September 2020 – Sharjeel Usmani is released on bail following the order of a Sessions Court in Aligarh.

8 September 2020 – KKM members Sagar Gorkhe and Ramesh Gaichor are arrested by the NIA in connection with the Bhima Koregaon case. Shortly after, they release a video statement alleging that the NIA tried to get them to be witnesses in the Bhima Koregaon case and pressured them to falsely admit to visiting Maoist leaders in a jungle in Gadchiroli.

9 September 2020 – KKM member Jyoti Jagtap is arrested by the NIA in connection with the Bhima Koregaon case.

13 September 2020 – Activist and co-founder of United Against Hate Umar Khalid is arrested in the FIR 59 conspiracy case.

14 September 2020 – A 19-year-old Dalit woman is gang-raped in Hathras district in UP by four dominant caste men. She dies of injuries two weeks later in a Delhi hospital. After her death, the body is forcibly cremated by the police without the consent of the family.

29 September 2020 – The Indian chapter of Amnesty International shuts down operations and lays off all staff after the Indian government froze its bank accounts.

5 October 2020 – Journalist Siddique Kappan, Campus Front of India activists Atikur Rahman and Masood Ahmad and driver Mohammad Alam are arrested by the UP Police on their way to Hathras to meet the family of the Dalit woman raped on 14 September.

8 October 2020 – 83-year-old Jesuit priest and Adivasi rights defender Father Stan Swamy is arrested in Ranchi.

10 October 2020 – A supplementary chargesheet is filed against the newly accused in the Bhima Koregaon case. Charges include Hany Babu's civil society efforts to get G.N. Saibaba released.

23 October 2020 – Mobile phone seller Faizan Khan is granted bail on merits by the High Court; the appeal against the bail is dismissed by the Supreme Court on 23 November 2020.

31 October 2020 – UP chief minister Yogi Adityanath announces a law to curb 'Love Jihad'. The draft ordinance is passed on 24 November 2020 as the UP Prohibition of Unlawful Religious Conversion Ordinance, 2020 and assented to by the governor on 28 November 2020.

November 2020–January 2021 – Numerous bail applications are rejected for all the accused in the Bhima Koregaon case. There is international outrage over the failure to provide Stan Swamy, who suffers from Parkinson's disease, a sipper and a straw.

12 January 2021 – Nodeep Kaur – a Dalit labour rights activist and member of the Mazdoor Adhikar Sangathan (MAS), a union of industrial workers actively supporting the 2020–21 Indian farmers' protest – is arrested for participating in a protest outside a factory in Kundli Industrial Area (KIA) on the outskirts of Delhi. She is beaten and sexually assaulted while in police custody.

24 January 2021 – Kanchan Nanavare dies in custody at the age of 37 following a serious case of medical negligence. She was arrested in 2014 for alleged Maoist connections and died awaiting trial.

30 January 2021 – Journalist Mandeep Punia is arrested by the Delhi Police at Singhu border while covering the farmers' protests. He is granted bail on 2 February 2021.

8 February 2021 – Boston-based Arsenal Consulting releases a forensic report proving that documents were planted into the hard drive of Rona Wilson's computer using malware. The American Bar Association expresses concern against the wrongful arrests of the BK16.

10 February 2021 – *The Washington Post* breaks the story of the forensic investigation and Wilson's lawyers file a case asking to quash the charges and appoint a Special Investigative Team to look into the planting of false evidence.

13 February 2021 – Disha Ravi, a climate change activist and a founder of Fridays For Future India, is arrested and charged with sedition for creating and sharing an online toolkit to support the ongoing farmers' protests. She will be granted bail on 23 February.

22 February 2021 – Varavara Rao is granted temporary medical bail. The decision to extend medical bail would be postponed for 14 months.

26 February 2021 – Nodeep Kaur is granted bail by the Punjab and Haryana High Courts.

9 March 2021 – Adivasi anti-mining activist Hidme Markam is arrested after the police register five FIRs against her with charges that include the UAPA. In the initial press release, the police accused Markam of being a Maoist and put a bounty of Rs. 100,000 (about 1,200 USD) on her.

4 May 2021 – The Delhi High Court issues show-cause notices for contempt of court to the Government of India for not meeting the Supreme Court's direction to supply 700 tonnes of medical-grade oxygen for hospitals in Delhi.

14 June 2021 – Asif Iqbal Tanha, Natasha Narwal and Devangana Kalita are granted bail on merit by the Delhi High Court. At the time of writing, the appeal is pending before the Supreme Court.

4 July 2021 – More than 80 Muslim women are put up for sale on auction online. Their photos and personal information are appropriated and uploaded on an open-source mobile application called Sulli Deals, offering users to claim a *sulli* – a derogatory term used for Muslim women – as deal of the day.

5 July 2021 – Father Stan Swamy dies in custody at the age of 84 for the consequences of medical neglect.

15 July 2021 – As part of PIL challenging the validity of Section 124A of the IPC, the Supreme Court expresses concern for the widespread misuse of sedition law and its lack of accountability. The plea submits that Section 124A is wholly unconstitutional and should be unequivocally and unambiguously struck down. On 16 July 2021, PUCL also files a plea challenging the law. In that same month, Patricia Mukhim, editor of *The Shillong Times*, and Anuradha Bhasin, owner of *Kashmir Times*, also move the Supreme Court challenging the constitutional validity of the sedition law saying that it will continue to 'haunt and hinder' the right to free speech and the freedom of the press.

18 July 2021 – The France-based media non-profit organisation Forbidden Stories accesses a leaked database of 50,000 telephone numbers that may have been targeted for surveillance by clients of Israeli company NSO Group's Pegasus spyware. Sixteen media organisations around the world reveal the names of people who were either persons of interest or forensically identified as having been targeted by the spyware. Those on the list include heads of state, political figures, activists, students, lawyers and journalists.

The Wire reveals the names of 161 people who are targets or potential targets for surveillance in India.

23 July 2021 – Justice S.S. Shinde of the Bombay High Court withdraws comments praising Father Stan Swamy after NIA contested that they would put the agency in a bad light.

26 October 2021 – During an ultra-right-wing Vishva Hindu Parishad rally organised in protest of attacks against Hindus in Bangladesh during Durga Puja, a mosque is vandalised, Muslim homes and shops are plundered and set on fire in the state of Tripura.

27 October 2021 – The Supreme Court sets up an independent investigation to look into the Pegasus scandal.

7 December 2021 – A mob of 500 Hindu extremists vandalises a Catholic missionary school in Madhya Pradesh even though school authorities had requested police protection before the attack.

1 January 2022 – Muslim girls in Udupi, Karnataka start a protest after holding a press conference claiming they were denied permission to enter classes for wearing the hijab. Protests would soon spread across Karnataka, with ABVP organising counter-demonstrations demanding permission to wear saffron shawls if the hijab is allowed. The Karnataka government orders the compulsory use of uniforms and bans the hijab in educational institutions. Several petitioners approach the High Court of Karnataka against the ban.

4 January 2022 – The Mumbai Police arrests Vishal Kumar Jha and Shweta Singh in connection with the Bulli Bai app – an application similar to Sulli Deals – which puts Muslim women on sale in an online auction. Two days later, the police also arrest Neeraj Bishnoi as the app's mastermind.

14 January 2022 – Activist Prashant Rahi and three others, who were accused by the Uttarakhand Police of being Maoists, are acquitted 14 years after their arrest as the case against them collapses.

14 March 2022 – Ishrat Jahan is granted bail in the FIR 59 conspiracy case.

15 March 2022 – Stating that the hijab is not an essential religious practice, the Karnataka High Court bans its use in schools across the state.

10 June 2022 – The Muslim community stage large protests across India to demand action against Nupur Sharma and Naveen Jindal for their derogatory remarks against Prophet Mohammad. More than 200 protesters are arrested from several cities.

11 June 2022 – Two youth, 14-year-old Mudasir and 19-year-old Sahil Ansari, are killed by the police shooting live ammunition against the protesting Muslim crowd in Ranchi. On the same day, Javed Mohammad, Welfare Party leader and father of activist Afreen Fatima, is named as one of the 'key conspirators' in the protests and arrested for instigating violence, while his wife and younger daughter are kept in police custody and released 24 hours later.

12 June 2022 – Javed Mohammad's house is surrounded by anti-riots squads and bulldozed by the Allahabad Police.

17 June 2022 – The UP government invokes the NSA, which allows for a detention for up to a year without charge or trial, against Javed Mohammad.

24 June 2022 – The Supreme Court, headed by Justice Khanwilkar, dismisses Zakia Jafri's pleas challenging the clean chit given by the Special Investigation Team to then Chief Minister Narendra Modi and others in the 2002 Gujarat pogrom.

25 June 2022 – The Gujarat Police register a case and then arrest former IPS officer Sanjiv Bhatt, former IPS officer R.B. Sreekumar and rights activist Teesta Setalvad for furnishing false information about the 2022 Gujarat pogrom. Bhatt was re-arrested from prison. He was first arrested in 2011 and sentenced to life in 2019 in a custodial death case during the Gujarat pogrom.

27 June 2022 – Fact-checker and journalist Mohammed Zubair is arrested by the Delhi Police weeks after he highlighted Nupur Sharma's derogatory comments about Prophet Mohammad. He is arrested under two sections of a law related to maintaining religious harmony for a 2018 Twitter post.

20 July 2022 – Inder Meghwal, a nine-year-old Dalit boy from Rajasthan, is beaten by a dominant caste teacher for touching an earthen pot of drinking water, he will die from the injuries on 13 August. On the same day, Mohammed Zubair is released on interim bail.

13 July 2022 – The Supreme Court presided by Justice Khanwilkar rejects the petition filed in 2009 for a probe into the extrajudicial killing of Chhattisgarh Adivasis and imposes a fine of Rs. 500,000 (about 6,000 USD) on the petitioner and social activist Himanshu Kumar.

10 August 2022 – Varavara Rao is granted medical bail.

25 August 2022 – Pandu Narote dies in custody supposedly for a case of swine flu. He was arrested along with G.N. Saibaba and sentenced to life by Gadchiroli District Court for aiding and abetting Maoist activities.

2 September 2022 – Teesta Setalvad is granted interim bail by the Supreme Court and released from Sabarmati Jail the next day.

9 September 2022 – Siddique Kappan is granted bail for charges under the UAPA, but remains in jail as a case probed by the Directorate of Enforcement is still pending.

19 September 2022 – Hany Babu is denied bail by the Bombay High Court noting that prima facie allegations against him are true and he was an active member of the banned CPI (Maoist).

28 September 2022 – The NIA Court begins hearing the discharge applications filed by seven of the BK16 who argue that charges against them are baseless. This is the first step towards framing of charges so the trial could begin almost four years after the case was registered.

29 September 2022 – The Supreme Court initially orders that Gautam Navlakha is released from prison and put under house arrest, but revises it after the solicitor-general opposes the order, saying he has not been able to look into the matter. The Court then orders that Navlakha is sent to hospital for check-up and treatment under police custody.

30 September 2022 – Sharjeel Imam is granted bail in the sedition case, but remains in jail for the two cases in connection with the 2020 Northeast Delhi violence.

14 October 2022 – The Nagpur Bench of the Bombay High Court acquits G.N. Saibaba and five others, who had been sentenced to life in 2017 for alleged Maoist links, citing absence of valid sanction under the UAPA.

15 October 2022 – With a special Saturday morning hearing, the Supreme Court convenes a two-judges bench and suspends the acquittal of G.N. Saibaba and five others and stays the release order issued by the Bombay High Court less than 24 hours earlier.

17 October 2022 – The Bombay High Court rejects KKM artist and activist Jyoti Jagtap's bail.

18 October 2022 – The Delhi High Court dismisses Umar Khalid's bail plea in the 2020 Northeast Delhi riots larger conspiracy case. Khalid had moved the Delhi High Court after he was denied bail by the Trial Court on 24 March.

18 November 2022 – The Bombay High Court grants bail to Anand Teltumbde.

19 November 2022 – Gautam Navlakha is released from jail and placed under house arrest for a period of one month.

25 November 2022 – The Supreme Court dismisses NIA's petition challenging the bail order and upholds the 18 November Bombay High Court's decision granting bail to Anand Teltumbde.

26 November 2022 – Anand Teltumbde is released from Taloja Central Jail in Navi Mumbai. He becomes the first person in the BK16 case to be granted bail on merits.

8 December 2022 – The results of the 2022 Gujarat Legislative Assembly Elections are declared: the BJP wins a seventh consecutive term with a record majority.

14 December 2022 – Forensic firm Arsenal Consulting finds evidence that the documents used to incriminate Father Stan Swamy were planted on his computer up to a week before the raid to his house that eventually led to his arrest and death in custody.

23 December 2022 – Umar Khalid gets bail for a week to attend his sister's wedding. On the same day, the Allahabad High Court grants bail to Siddique Kappan in a money laundering case; because of uncertainty over his surety, he will only be released on 2 February 2023.

27 December 2022 – Retired Sub-Divisional Police Officer Ganesh More – one of the main investigators in the BK16 case – declares under oath that they had no evidence to connect the Elgar Parishad meeting with the violence that took place at Bhima Koregaon.

2
Wages of Impunity:
Cracking Down on Dissent[1]

I was implicated in false cases. I had to fight for over a decade to prove myself innocent. I was a school teacher ... these false cases ruined my life, my dignity and my family had to suffer. Who will bring back my dignity and 11 years of my life lost in fighting against false charges? Can the state government or the Centre return it? It is not only about Soni Sori, as several tribals of Bastar region have been bearing the brunt of such false cases.

– Soni Sori, Adivasi school teacher turned political leader,
Dantewada, south Bastar

WAGING WAR AGAINST THE STATE

In May 2014, in what looked like a scene from a movie, a van pulled in front of Delhi University English professor G.N. Saibaba's car. The police from Gadchiroli, in plain clothes, dragged the driver out, then assaulted, blindfolded and kidnapped Saibaba from the university campus in broad daylight. No warrant was issued and he wasn't allowed to call his wife or lawyer. His wife, Vasantha, waiting for him to return home for lunch, found out about his abduction from an anonymous phone call. The following day Saibaba was flown out of Delhi and taken to the remote Aheri Police Station on the border between Maharashtra and Chhattisgarh. Here the district magistrate heard the case and sent Saibaba – who contracted polio as a child, is 90 per cent physically disabled

---

1. The title is borrowed from lawyer, scholar and activist K.G. Kannabiran's groundbreaking book *The Wages of Impunity: Power, Justice and Human Rights.* Orient Blackswan, 2018.

and wheelchair-bound – to prison, where he would spend the next 14 months in an *anda* cell (a small egg-shaped cell in a high security prison) in darkness.

G.N. Saibaba and five others – JNU student Hem Keshavdatta Mishra, journalist Prashant Rahi, members of Adivasi communities Mahesh Tirki, Pandu Narote and Vijay Nan Tirki – were charged with conspiring to 'wage war against India'.

Long before his arrest, G.N. Saibaba was hounded by the Indian state. Since 2013, the Delhi Police had raided his faculty residence on campus, searched its premises and interrogated him on

Suhas P. Bawache
Investigating Officer
Aheri Police Station
Gadchiroli
Maharashtra.

12/09/2013

This is to inform you that you must allow my lawyer in the process of the search of my house. Without the presence of my lawyer, I have a right to not allow you to search my house. You should take the permission from the university before you search my house. My current residence and my family privacy is being grossly voilated. Our phones were taken away and we were not allowed to talk to my colleagues and lawyers.

I have in clear terms expressed to you this objection several times. Inspite of this, you have not allowed my colleagues or my lawyer to be present in this search.

G. N. Saibaba
(Dr. G. N. SAIBABA)
Warden's Flat, Gwyer Hall
University Road, Delhi University
Delhi - 110 007

four different occasions. In one of these raids, over 50 police and intelligence officers stormed into his home and detained his entire family in different rooms, including his visibly frightened teenage daughter and the driver. During the raid, the police refused G.N. Saibaba access to his lawyer. The search warrant, finally produced after much pleading, was issued by Judicial Magistrate N.G. Vyas, who allowed the police to 'recover stolen property' from Saibaba's home. However, the warrant had no basis in law and the late S.A.R. Geelani, the then President of the Committee for the Release of Political Prisoners, called it a 'figment of imagination'.[2]

When the police left their ransacked home after three hours, they had seized pen drives, hard drives, photographs, laptops, phone SIM cards and mobile phones. The hard drives had personal photos, videos of protests and Saibaba's manuscripts. The 'seizure list' resembled a reading list for social movements rather than items that would suggest a 'conspiracy to incite violence' by a mastermind. It included booklets and magazines, old copies of *People's March* magazine, a booklet on the killing of Naxal leader Kishenji, material from *Arunatara* magazine published by Revolutionary Writers Association, Andhra Pradesh and issues of *Jan Pratirodh* magazine published by Revolutionary Democratic Front. In violation of procedural rules, during the search the police used plastic bags from the couple's kitchen to carry away the seized material without sealing them in evidence bags. When the police finally returned some of their photos, one of Saibaba's prized possessions – a photograph of him with Kenyan writer Ngugi wa Thiong'o – was missing. In an interview soon after, Saibaba joked: 'They probably thought Ngugi's a Maoist.'[3] On second thought, they probably did.

The whispers of his arrest were in the air long before he was abducted.

Saibaba was the spokesperson for the campaign against Operation Green Hunt. In 2005, the Indian government started a counter-insurgency campaign in Chhattisgarh and in 2009 it

---

2. Press statement from teachers of Delhi University, 'Statements against police raid at GN Saibaba's house.' *Sanhati*, 13 September 2013.

3. Shreya Roy Chowdhury, 'G N Saibaba: the revolutionary in Delhi University.' *The Times of India*, 26 September 2013.

launched Operation Green Hunt.[4] While the official mandate was to eliminate the Naxalite militants, it was an all-out war on the Adivasi communities in India's mineral-rich 'Red Corridor'.[5] In 2010, journalist Aman Sethi wrote: 'An operation is underway in Central India, but no one knows what it is ... away from the gaze of the media and the judiciary, the Adivasis of Bastar are paying a heavy price ... for just being there.'[6]

Adivasi lands were confiscated, entire villages were emptied and communities were driven out. Saibaba travelled and visited 'almost every Adivasi district' with community members, who carried him 'on shoulders ... up to the hilly forests'.[7] At the end of his extensive travels, he concluded that Operation Green Hunt 'was launched to kill, maim and dislodge these people'. Others echoed his observations: 'In the name of development, a cultural genocide is being carried out against the Adivasis: a slow death of everything that made their lives meaningful.'[8] Destruction of Adivasi homes was called development, while any resistance to it was labelled Naxal, Maoist or anti-national.

In June 2011, the Sanhati Collective published a list of 195 victims of Operation Green Hunt in Chhattisgarh since August 2009 when it was first launched, with names, ages and the circumstances surrounding the killings.[9] Last updated on 1 June 2011, the list remains incomplete, many incidents of killings and disappearances unreported and, in other cases, the witnesses themselves have disappeared or have been killed.

---

4.   Adolfo Naya Fernández, Operation 'Green Hunt' in India: Social practices of the genocidal counter-insurgency strategy 'Hearts and minds.' *Foreign Languages Press*, 2020.
5.   The Red Corridor includes the states of Chhattisgarh, Jharkhand, Odisha, Bihar and West Bengal. The operation would later expand to Andhra Pradesh, Telangana and Maharashtra.
6.   Aman Sethi, 'Green Hunt: the anatomy of an operation.' *The Hindu*, 6 February 2010.
7.   Mehboob Jeelani, 'The best way to stop me was to throw me in jail, says Saibaba.' *The Hindu*, 6 July 2015.
8.   Felix Padel and Samarendra Das, *Anthropology of a Genocide: Tribal Movements in Central India against Over-industrialisation*. SAAG, 2006.
9.   Sanhati Collective, 'List of victims of Operation Green Hunt in Chhattisgarh since August 2009.' *Sanhati*, 13 June 2011.

Date	No. of People Killed	Name	Sex/Age	Native Village	Site of killing	Block/ District	How were they killed?
10-Aug-09	6	Oyam Sagar	M/30	Vecham	Vecham		All were caught and shot dead. Out of them the only girl Somli was an unarmed member of the peoples' militia. Rest were innocent peasants
		Emla Pandru	M/25	Choukanpal	Choukanpal		
		Hapka Lingu	M/25	"	"	Bijapur	
		Tati Lakmu	M/25	Etepadu	Etepadu		
		Tati Aitu	M/45	"	"		
		Karam Somli	F/16	Timmenar	Timmenar		
13-Aug-09	2	Madkam Sannu	M/45	Keshmundi		Bhairamgarh/Bijapur	Killed in fake encounter
		Podiyam Somdu	M/30	"			
7-Sep-09	1	Kunjam Bhima	M	Duvvalkarka	Duvvalkarka	Dantewada	caught and shot dead
7-Sep-09	1	Madkam Raju	M/20	Timmenar		Bijapur	caught and shot dead
8-Sep-09	4	Sodi Sona	M/55	Gollagudem	Gollagudem	Dantewada	caught and shot dead but encounter not declared
		Sodi Bheemal	M/45				
		Sodi Aite	F/25				
		Madivi Deval	M/50				
13-Sep-09	1	Kavasi Sukram	M/25	Keskuttul		Bijapur	caught and shot dead
17-Sep-09	1	Madivi Deval	M/30	Singanmadugu	Singanmadugu	Dantewada	caught and killed in cold blood and not declared
17-Sep-09	5	Dudi Muye	F/70	Gachanpally	Gachanpally	Dantewada	caught and killed in cold blood and not declared
		Madivi Adamal	M/45				
		Madakam Chulal	M/45				
		Madivi Jogal	M/60				
		Madivi Gangal	M/70				beaten unto death and not declared
17-Sep-09	5	Paddem Deval	M/25	Gattampadu	Between Nallabelly and Gollapally villages	Dantewada	caught and killed in cold blood
		Dudi Pojjal	M/15				
		Sodi Masal	M/20				
		Tuniki Sinnal	M/35				
		Sodi Shanesh	M/43	Palachelma			
17-Sep-09	1	Dudi Adamal	M/35		Paidagudem		

G.N. Saibaba mobilised writers, students and various groups under the Forum Against War on People. Saibaba's gravest crime was that he was becoming effective and the campaign was beginning to show results. Saibaba recalled being warned on multiple occasions. He once remarked: 'The best way to stop me was to throw me in jail.'[10]

Finally, after 14 months of imprisonment, Saibaba was given bail on medical grounds by the Bombay High Court in June 2015. However, the Court's Nagpur Bench cancelled his bail in December of the same year and he had to return to prison.

THERE WAS NO CRIME, NO EVIDENCE

During the three-year-long trial against Saibaba and the five others, the prosecution produced no real evidence. Of 23 witnesses presented before the court by the prosecution, 22 were police officers. The only civilian witness retracted his confession after claiming it resulted from torture. While Saiababa's health deteriorated in prison, Prashant Rahi, Hem Mishra, Pandu Narote and Mahesh Tirki were tortured in custody by investigating officer Suhas Bawache.

---

10. Jeelani, 'The best way to stop me was to throw me in jail, says Saibaba.'

The prosecution's case was wholly based on the 'confessions' extracted from Mahesh Tirki and Pandu Narote under torture. Yet, despite affidavits filed by both alleging the brutal conditions under which the statements were made, the judge refused to believe them and admitted the confessions in contravention of the law of evidence. The evidence mounted by the state against Saibaba and others consisted of letters, newspapers, umbrellas, pamphlets, books on Marxism and videos seized during searches, whose legality the defence repeatedly challenged.

The prosecution alleged that Saibaba operated under 'various aliases' and was a 'kingpin' of the Maoist insurgents. However, there was no evidence that Saibaba or the others had 'any role to play in any violence or incitement to violence or any active participation at all' and no weapons were found or recovered.

Many who witnessed the trial saw it as a farce in action, a badly written and poorly executed fiction staged by the prosecution. Saibaba and his lawyer Surendra Gadling believed the courts would acquit him. Instead, in an 827-page judgment, Suryakant Shinde, the judge at Gadchiroli District Court, convicted G.N. Saibaba and the five others for conspiring to wage war against India. Saibaba's defence committee called the judgment 'Terminator-like' and 'accelerating [the] annihilation of voices of resistance.'[11]

Five of the accused were sentenced to life, while Vijay Nan Tirki was sentenced to ten years. At the time of the judgment in 2017, Saibaba was 47; Hem Mishra 32; Prashant Rahi 54; Mahesh Tirki 22; Pandu Narote 27; and Vijay Nan Tirki 30.

Throughout the judgment, Shinde's dislike for the men, and in particular for Saibaba, was evident. He declared that 'merely because ... Saibaba is 90% disabled is no grounds to show him leniency.'[12] During his first 14 months in prison, Saibaba's health deteriorated considerably, his left hand became paralysed and he

---

11.   Tekendra Parmar, 'The persecution of GN Saibaba and India's "annihilation" of the resistance.' *The Nation*, 3 May 2018.

12.   Ipsita Chakravarty, 'A chilling judgment sentences Delhi academician GN Saibaba to life in prison.' *Scroll.in*, 8 March 2017.

was taken to hospital 27 times.[13] It was as if they did everything to deplete his spirit.

How did the prosecution succeed in getting the professor and five others convicted of 'waging war against the nation' without presenting credible evidence?

Shinde remarked that the situation of Gadchiroli district since the 1980s was 'paralyzed' with 'no industrial and other developments' because of 'Naxals' and their 'violence'. And added: 'Hence, in my opinion, imprisonment for life is also not sufficient punishment for the accused.'

Gadchiroli is as much a story of mines and militarisation as it is one of resistance. Locals have sustained decades-long resistance and remained determined to protect their lands, livelihoods and gods that government and corporations are keen to grab from them. The cost of resistance was paid in blood and toil – police raids, interrogations, arrests, torture, rape and disappearances became the everyday reality alongside the destruction of livelihoods. A report on 'encounter killing', where the state massacred 40 people including children in the name of capturing Maoists, summarises what was happening in Gadchiroli:

> Each was a tribal, a local person of the area, and a citizen of the country. The elders of their families have fought invaders who have threatened to take away their land, livelihood, and dignity. Now, they fight the invasion of the 'state' that is hell-bent on wooing corporate interests, which are in violent contradiction to the interests of the people of the land.[14]

Shinde essentially decided that the crime was that of speaking, protesting and political activism, which in his opinion had stalled 'development' and was deserving of life in prison. Activist and journalist Gautam Navlakha, in an interview citing the judge's

---

13. Pavan Dahat, 'Govt. wanted to kill me: Saibaba.' *The Hindu*, 8 April 2016.
14. See the full report by a 40-member fact-finding team that visited the area between 5 and 7 May 2018: Coordination of Democratic Rights Organisations, IAPL and Women Against Sexual Violence and State Repression, *Encountering Resistance: State Policy for Development in Gadchiroli. People's Union for Democratic Rights*, 2018.

observation, said that 'left to himself, [Shinde] would have preferred the death penalty' for these men.[15]

Mahesh Tirki's gravest offence was possessing pamphlets – Naxal literature that opposed the Surjagarh iron mining project, Operation Green Hunt and a pamphlet condemning the Khairlanji massacre – the brutal rape and murder of a Dalit family – and the Maharashtra government's role in protecting the perpetrators of the killings. The judge interpreted these pamphlets as 'incriminating articles' and evidence of waging war. He concluded that the mere possession was indicative of 'showing hatred towards the government'. In the judgment, Shinde lists without irony various 'incriminating articles:'

> From the possession of accused no.1 Mahesh Tirki, three pamphlets containing Naxal literature and from the possession of no.2 Pandu Narote the articles like umbrella and newspaper usually used by Naxal as identification code to recognize each other were seized.

Lawyer Rebecca John commented that 'Saibaba has been convicted for his ideology.'[16] Under existing laws, one cannot be convicted unless they are found to have committed a crime. However, under the UAPA convicting and condemning anyone based on their thoughts had become a possibility.

In 2011, while providing bail to activist Dr Binayak Sen, the Supreme Court ruled that possession of Maoist literature does not make one Maoist. It stated that 'mere membership of a banned organisation would not make a person criminally liable unless he resorts to violence or incites people to violence or creates public disorder by violence or incitement to violence.'[17] In May 2015, the

---

15. Newsclick Staff, 'G.N. Saibaba being persecuted for his ideas? by Gautam Navlakha.' *NewsClick*, 14 March 2017.

16. Shoaib Daniyal, 'Saibaba conviction: how a draconian law has turned mere thought into crime.' *Scroll.in*, 9 March 2017.

17. The Supreme Court cited its previous decision in *Arup Bhuyan* v. *State of Assam*, delivered on 3 February 2011 in this judgment. The Court relied on US judgments dating back to the 1960s including the landmark *Clarence Brandenburg* v. *State of Ohio*, 1969.

Kerala High Court ordered that 'being a Maoist is not a crime' and a person can be prosecuted only when they have acted unlawfully while pursuing the Maoist line.[18]

The settled law is that possession of Maoist literature or supporting an ideology is not considered a crime or an abetment of crime. Yet Shinde, who sentenced Saibaba and others to life imprisonment, wrongly ruled that this judgment did not apply in this case.

We asked a lawyer who assisted Gadling in the case if, in retrospect, something could have been done differently.[19] He said no:

The judge had made up his mind that these men should not exist anymore. They don't like people like Saibaba or Gadling. [India] is a caste colony. Seeing politically assertive people, especially Dalits, Adivasis or Muslims, makes these people very uncomfortable. It was not about the law; it was about hate. And they are writing blank checks for the corporation to do anything, so they had to remove all and any obstacles.

The state was essentially working for the corporations against its own people. The lawyer said that most judges he encounters hold on to hate like a prize and 'you can see it in the judgments they pass.' This was not a judicial decision based on evidence, laws, facts or established legal precedents; it was wholly based on the

---

18.   The Supreme Court ordered the release on bail of activist Binayak Sen, who was convicted and sentenced on charges of sedition in 2010 by the Chhattisgarh High Court, during the pendency of the appeal against his conviction. Sen appealed the High Court order before the Supreme Court. The Supreme Court allowed Sen's appeal but did not explain the reasoning. Some speculated that the judgment was grounded in the belief that charges against Sen were unfounded. However, in March 2023, the Supreme Court set aside its own judgments that 'mere membership' of an unlawful association or organisation did not make a person a criminal or a terrorist. The three-judge bench of the Supreme Court, headed by Justice M.R. Shah ruled that 'to punish a person who is a member of such an unlawful association is in furtherance of the objective of effective prevention of unlawful incidents' and observed that 'fundamental rights are not absolute'. This decision expands the already unfettered power of the Indian state and its security agencies to incarcerate anyone based on a mere allegation of 'unlawful membership'. The ruling has now effectively made dissent treason.
19.   All the lawyers we interviewed spoke on condition of anonymity for their own safety and the safety of their clients.

presumptions, conjectures, prejudices and predilections of Justice Shinde. In his opinion, books, pamphlets, BBC documentaries and video recordings were sufficient to suggest that Saibaba and others were guilty of waging war against the mighty Indian state.

A bookshelf was now evidence of sedition.

What gives a judge the impunity to trample established principles of law and eagerly rule without considerations of proportionality, reasonableness or due process?

Indian judges have been increasingly using jingoistic language in defence of indefensible judgments that run contrary to the law and the fundamental principles enshrined in the Constitution. Rather than interpret rights and principles in favour of citizens, they have increasingly become an extension, as ideological foot soldiers or stenographers, of an authoritarian state.

The vast power granted under the UAPA and the regimes of impunity it offers have fundamentally remade what it means to disagree with the Indian state. The UAPA essentially reversed criminal law by shifting the burden of proof from the prosecution to the defence and making it illegal to hold certain political beliefs, especially those that question the Indian state. The Indian courts show deep authoritarian tendencies and their jurisprudence increasingly manifests inflexibility and lack of compassion, providing a tacit approval of the ongoing oppression.

CREATING THE TEMPLATE FOR PERSECUTION: THE CASE OF BINAYAK SEN

Saibaba is not the first scholar and human rights defender to be arrested under the UAPA using fabricated charges – before him there were Binayak Sen, Soni Sori, Gaur Chakraborty, Sudhir Dawale, Arun Ferreira, Kobad Ghandy. The list is long: for every activist whose name is remembered, recorded and their case reported, hundreds disappear. In 2010 alone, seven civil society activists and writers were charged with sedition. That year, for example, E. Rati Rao, vice-president of the Karnataka chapter of the PUCL, was issued a sedition notice for publishing a privately circulated news bulletin that was discontinued three years before.

Yet, the decision in Saibaba's case marks the beginning of a new period of lawless justice. So what changed? Professor Saroj Giri writes that 'they [the state] got greedier, more demanding'.[20] After successfully capturing and killing Maoist leaders like Azad and Kishenji during peace talks, Giri argued that they now had their eyes set on the 'pigeons'. Mihir Desai, one of the defence lawyers in the Bhima Koregaon case, used the metaphor of a lion having tasted human blood: 'First, with the case of Binayak Sen and Saibaba, they tasted blood, and now [in 2018–20] they are going all out'.[21]

For over three decades, Dr Binayak Sen ran a mobile clinic training health workers in one of Chhattisgarh's areas most affected by the Maoist insurgency. In 2005, as the head of PUCL, he documented deaths due to hunger and malnutrition and the displacement of over 600 Adivasi villages by the Salwa Judum, a state-sponsored militia, which Human Rights Watch called 'a state-supported vigilante group aimed at eliminating Naxalites'.[22] Two years later, in 2007, he was accused of being a *Naxali daakiya* (a postman for the Naxalites), arrested and charged with sedition for his visits to Raipur prison (approved by the jail authorities) to meet the Marxist ideologue Narayan Sanyal. He was charged with waging a war against the state with a list of the most surreal evidence.[23]

What is alarming is not that the prosecution and the police fabricated charges and presented innocuous objects and materials as evidence; the concern is that the lower court disregarded the law and relied on faulty evidence, half-truths and lies to convict Binayak Sen and sentence him to life. The Chhattisgarh High Court, agreeing with the lower court, rejected his appeal for suspension of the sentence and grant of bail. It concluded that 'Sen was found in possession of documents that attempted to incite hatred and disaffection toward the lawfully established govern-

20. Saroj Giri, 'The Bhima Koregaon arrests and the resistance in India.' *Monthly Review*, 12 November 2022.
21. Ibid.
22. John Emerson, 'Being neutral is our biggest crime.' *Human Rights Watch*, 25 June 2015.
23. People's Union for Civil Liberties, 'Analysis of the case against Dr. Binayak Sen.' *PUCL*, 21 July 2007.

ANNEXURE I: LIST OF THE SEIZED DOCUMENTS FROM DR. BINAYAK SEN'S HOUSE:

Although the police was claiming in front of the media on 19th May 2007 immediately after the house search that they had found some significant documents, a copy of the seizure memo enlisting all the material exposes the "white lie" of the police. These are as follows:

1. Five CDs, mostly pertaining to the various investigations regarding Fake Encounters in Gollapalli, Katgaon, Surguja, and Jharkhand, which were made during the PUCL investigations, and contain interviews with the concerned citizens. PUCL has been distributing these for the last two years.

2. The Computer CPU, yet to be examined by experts;

3. A post-card dated 3.6.2006 written to Dr. Binayak Sen by the CPI (Maoist) leader, Sri Narayan Sanyal lodged at the Raipur Central Jail, regarding his health as well as legal case, which is duly signed by the Jail authorities carrying the Seal of the Jail Authorities;

4. News-paper clippings dated 19.6.2006, 8.4.2006, 27.8.2006, 26.12.2006, 21.8.2006, 8.1.2007, 21.12.2006 (Total 10 paper cuttings)

5. A Yellow coloured booklet "ON THE UNITY BETWEEN CPI (Peoples' War) AND MAOIST COMMUNIST CENTRE" in Hindi

6. A Letter written by Madanlal Banjare (a member of the CPI- Maoist) from Jail addressed to "Priya Comrade Binayak Sen" revealing the inhuman conditions and illegal activities in Raipur Central Jail.

(OUR NOTE: This letter was later sent to all newspapers and electronic media by the PUCL, and was prominently published in some newspapers);

7. A Xeroxed Article in English entitled: "Naxal Movement, Tribals and Women's Movement"

(OUR NOTE: This Article is based on a dialogue carried out in Andhra Pradesh during the period of the Peace Talks and was later published in the prestigious periodical Economic and Political Weekly, Mumbai)

8. A hand written photocopied note of 4 pages on "How to build an Anti-US Imperialist Front.";

9. Eight page Article entitled: "KRANTIKARI JANWADI MORCHA (ITF) VAISHAVIKARAN AWAM BAHRTIYE SEVA KSHETRA: (Globalization and the Service Sector in India)

10. A recent document dated 18.7.06 of CPI (M) "Recent Police Activities and Labourers". B.10;

11. A Book on 'SALWA JUDUM: Bastar ki janata par Fasivadi hamla published by the Committee of Tribals affected by Salwa Juroom (48 pages); in which on page number 41 is a Press Release Maowadiyon aur Bhautiki Jan Samsayayon par Jari Barbarta sarkaar prayojit Salwa Judum ka Virodh Karo dated 11th March 2006 (One page);

ment' – a reminder that not a single material was produced against Sen to prove that he was involved in propagating Maoist ideology.

The Supreme Court, in an appeal, finally suspended the sentence and released him on bail. Justice Prasad said: 'We are a democratic country. He may be a sympathizer. That does not make him guilty of sedition.'[24] However, the damage was done. What the state learned in the Binayak Sen case, they perfected with the trial of G.N. Saibaba, incarcerating along the way Sudhir Dhawale, Soni Sori and countless others.

The argument that 'the judiciary is the bulwark of democracy' can be easily reversed: the judiciary can promptly become the arm shepherding deeply authoritarian tendencies and can quickly redefine and remake what justice means.

Law is often punitive, oppressive, violent and a well-honed arm that justifies state violence. It is essential to understand that the UAPA and the entire infrastructure of terror laws are legislated to be tyrannical by design and not by exception. It is often said that the law defines the offence and the state the offender. Today the figure of the questioning and rights-bearing citizen has become an 'enemy of the state' to be eliminated. This trail of legal cases, judicial apathy and decisions has created a template that is now regularly used as in the arrests of Bhima Koregaon activists, in connection with the Delhi violence and against journalists and activists who went to cover the Hathras rape and murder. They all have been labelled as 'anti-national' and 'Urban Naxals' and falsely accused of Maoist links. This label has enabled the filing of terror and sedition charges against all of them, making indefinite detention the norm, with the near impossibility of getting bail.

Sen's trial was a farce and Saibaba's conviction a tragedy – a frightening moment, a precursor, one of the many omens of the purge to come. Almost everyone who campaigned against Operation Green Hunt in Chhattisgarh has since been arrested. Similarly, many members of the Committee for the Defence and Release of G.N. Saibaba – Anand Teltumbde, Hany Babu, Rona Wilson, Sudhir Dhawale and even his lawyer Surendra Gadling – have been arrested.

---

24.   J. Venkatesan, 'Binayak Sen gets bail in Supreme Court.' *The Hindu*, 15 April 2011.

THE ARTIST BECOMES THE TERRORIST

Vilas Ghogre was a revolutionary Dalit poet, a bard, an artist and an activist. In 1997 with a blue bandana tied around his head, he hung himself in protest against the gruesome massacre at the hands of police officer Manohar Kadam, who killed ten people and injured 25 others in Ramabai Nagar, a predominantly Dalit colony. His suicide note was written on the walls of his modest home in Mulund and it read: 'I cannot withstand this injustice. So I'm committing suicide as a mark of protest and *Ambedkarwadi Ekjuta Zindabad* (Hail Ambedkarite Unity)!'[25]

The state-sanctioned murder of civilians, the ruthless suppression of dissent and the impunity enjoyed by the police to kill and maim Dalits are not an aberration. It is a story of repression and impunity perfected over time. Seven years after the Ramabai Nagar killings, the police filed charges of 'attempted murder' against those injured and claimed that the officers had indiscriminately opened fire on civilians at a close range in self-defence. After a decade-long struggle for justice, court battles and appeals, Manohar Kadam was finally found guilty, but instead of being jailed, he was released on bail in 2009. In the aftermath of this verdict, Anand Teltumbde (who would soon be arrested) wrote a searing critique of how the Indian 'State had zealously sheltered its petty minion, Manohar Kadam'. While in sharp contrast, 'arrested Binayak Sen ... without even an iota of evidence against him'.[26]

For Teltumbde, the state treats Dalits and Adivasis as

> [the] primordial marker of our intrinsically uncivil caste society which feigns civility for itself ... Unfortunately, the modern constitutional State that we created, instead of doing away with this 'un-civility', the modern constitutional State that we created has itself imbibed it in full measure, promoting and accentuating

25. Anupama Rao, 'Stigma and labour: remembering Dalit Marxism'. *Seminar*, Issue 633, May 2012. Prasanna D. Zorey, 'Dalit poet commits suicide in protest'. *Rediff*, date not listed.
26. Anand Teltumbde, 'How the state treats friends and foes of the oppressed'. *Economic and Political Weekly*, 44 (25), 20 June 2009.

this divide ... [The] State apparatus favors those against Dalits and tribals and vice versa. If you sympathize with Dalits and tribals, you become an outcast, but if you despise them, you get naturally accepted. Naxalism and nationalism ... [have] become modern-day euphemistic epithets for outcaste and caste, respectively.[27]

THE STATE HAS ITS BOOTS ON THE NECK

A Dalit activist we spoke to said that most people do not encounter the state the way Dalits, Adivasis and Muslims do. She told us: 'The state has always had a boot on our necks.' Forget living; imagine what it takes to survive this. The boot is always pressed against minorities' necks, making it hard to breathe, demanding that they beg for dignity every day. She added: '[For us] it doesn't matter who is in power; oppression is the only thing that hasn't changed'.

Like Vilas Ghogre and other poets and revolutionary bards who have used poetry as an anti-caste tool, KKM – an artists' collective set up in the wake of the 2002 Gujarat pogrom – follows this tradition.

After the Ramabai Nagar's firing, the Khairlanji massacre became another critical moment in Dalit political mobilisation. It took months for the news to spread and none of the mainstream media reported on the massacre. Dalit organisations mobilised, protested, filed petitions and, by the end of the year, photographs of the victims' bodies were pasted on the walls of Dalit *bastis*. The state quickly swung into action and police cover-ups and bureaucratic mishandling made justice impossible. Anupama Rao, in the aftermath of the massacre, pointed to the state's fear of the 'Dalit rage' as 'for the state machinery ... the violence of Khairlanji was quickly substituted by the threat of Dalit counterviolence'.[28] The state saw any form of Dalit challenge to institutionalised discrimination and resistance against violence or indignity as a source of

---

27.   Ibid.
28.   Anupama Rao, 'Violence and humanity: or, vulnerability as political subjectivity'. *Social Research: An International Quarterly*, 78 (4), 2011: 607–32.

concern. These acts were quickly labelled as counterviolence to be crushed immediately.

KKM lead singer Sheetal Sathe said that they 'could not fathom the brutality of that massacre.'[29] Deepak Dhengle said that the gruesome event and the anger that followed transformed KKM's songs, politics and life. After Khairlanji, the atrocities just kept increasing and inspired their songs 'De Dalita Thoka' (Fight back Dalits!) and 'Dalits, Hala Bol' (Dalits, get ready): 'This democracy is not for you; / This judiciary is not for you. / This judiciary is not for you; / this governance is not for you.'[30]

KKM asked simple yet powerful questions through their songs and performances. 'If we can't speak our minds, then what is the use of this democracy? No one wants to talk about our rights.' As their popularity grew, the Congress-led Maharashtra state government published in local newspapers a 'hit list' of 37 organisations and activists, including KKM, labelling them as Naxalites.

The police put the group under surveillance, started turning up at their events and homes while their book stalls were raided and their books seized. In 2011, Deepak Dhengle and Siddharth Bhosle were arrested under terror laws and Sheetal Sathe, Sagar Gorkhe, Ramesh Gaichor and Sachin Mali were forced underground after threats from the police. In 2013, they finally re-emerged and gave themselves up to the state after Dhengle and Bhosle were released on bail. Sathe (who was pregnant), Mali, Gorkhe and Gaichor were immediately imprisoned and their bail rejected twice. Sathe was granted bail in late 2013 on humanitarian grounds when she was almost eight-and-a-half months into her pregnancy, while the other three languished in jail for four more years until they were finally released in 2017.

Dhengle, in custody, was tortured, beaten, stripped, his hands and legs tied with a rope and hung from the ceiling. In an interview, he joked that the judge who granted bail to the Bollywood

29. Rasika Ajotikar, 'Our song impure, our voice polluted': conversations with activist and musician Shital Sathe.' Feminist Review, 119, 2018: 154–62.
30. Sonam Singh, Forbidden Notes | Documentary Film about Arrests of Kabir Kala Manch Members, 2016. All the following KKM members' quotes are from the documentary.

superstar Salman Khan after a deadly hit-and-run conviction was the same judge who denied bail to all the KKM members for over two years, adding: 'No one knows how long this case will drag on.' Between 2011 and 2015, the state couldn't produce a single witness against Dhengle, who asked: 'They label us Naxalites if we talk about farmer suicide and malnourishment ... We talk about Dalit issues and that of the backward classes. So why do they have to arrest us for this?'

Why did the state go after a cultural protest group? When songs and street play are weapons and artists become terrorists, what does it say about the state? What is the state hiding? Who is it silencing? As a Dalit activist we spoke to put it:

They have always come for us first. They have killed our people ... This is what I mean: it seems unbelievable when they come for intellectuals, writers, lawyers and thinkers now. But what is unbelievable in your world has always been our everyday reality. The state always comes for us and there is always a noose connected to us that can be tightened any time.

Dalit social activist and editor of *Vidrohi*, Sudhir Dhawale was arrested in 2011 for his alleged links with the Maoists. After three years in prison, he was acquitted of all charges. On his release, he said:

Dissenting voices are stifled. We rarely see the oppressed caste fight back. The sustained agitation we saw post-Khairlanji [against caste atrocities] is no longer a common sight. Many of us who participated in protest rallies then have been booked in cases. We were labeled as 'Naxals.'[31]

The state's need to silence the Naxal threat and the Dalit rage are inextricably linked. The Indian state has always resorted to illegal measures to deal with the Naxalite threat, including extrajudicial

---

31. Anand Teltumbde, 'Labelling Dalits and Adivasis as Maoists is an old state strategy for crushing dissent and criticism.' Excerpt from *Republic of Caste*, Scroll. *in*, 7 June 2018.

executions, torture and forced disappearances.[32] Most victims of these police abuses are labourers and peasants from Adivasi and Dalit communities.

Often singled out as Naxalite sympathisers, attacks on rural activists and labourers are sanctioned as part of a campaign to fight Naxalite terrorism. In India's new national security state, police officers possess absolute and unfettered powers over life and death. Senior police officers with a record of killing Adivasi and peasants regularly receive promotions, cash rewards and favourable postings. The system that has institutionalised lawlessness also rewards exceptional brutality. Long before KKM was implicated in the Bhima Koregaon violence, they were already hounded.

Justice Abhay Thipsay of the Bombay High Court, granting bail to Deepak Dhengle, held the rights to freedom of speech, assemble peacefully and form associations in primacy over the UAPA: 'Speaking about corruption, social inequality, exploitation of the poor, etc. and desiring that a better society should come in existence is not banned in our country. Claiming that these wrongs exist in our society cannot be banned and made punishable.'[33]

This act of gathering, protesting and even of speaking about peace would be penalised very soon. The worst was yet to come.

ELGAR PARISHAD AND THE MAKING OF THE BK16 POLITICAL PRISONERS

On 31 December 2017, the Elgar Parishad – a meeting with over 35,000 people forming an anti-caste and anti-fascist front – took place in Pune. The following day, many of those present at the gathering, along with thousands of Dalits, attended the celebration of the 200th anniversary of the battle of Koregaon. In a premeditated attack, a right-wing Hindu nationalist mob carrying saffron flags attacked the celebration and the violence soon spread to the nearby villages. Ramdas Lokhande, a local reporter, saw men in the village

---

32. Grace Pelly, 'State terrorism: torture, extra-judicial killings, and forced disappearances in India: report of the Independent People's Tribunal.' Socio Legal Information Centre, 9–10 February 2008.

33. Geetanjali Gurlhosur, 'Kabir Kala Manch: a history of revolutionary singing and state repression.' Ritimo, 7 April 2022.

prepare the ground for violence, calling it a 'well-planned riot' where 'everything was systematically planned'.[34] Local anti-caste activist Anita Sawale described the violence she encountered: 'I had witnessed the violence up close. People all around me were beaten up and soaked in blood. Our vehicles were burnt, and the attackers openly chanted slogans hailing their leaders, Bhide and Ekbote.'[35]

The next day Sawale filed a case against Hindutva leader Milind Ekbote – who is often referred to as *Dharmaveda Mathefiru* (crazy religious fanatic) – and Sambhaji Bhide for the attack. Despite threats to her life, Sawale continued to fight for those affected by the violence, including filing a petition with the Bombay High Court demanding accountability.

Protesting the violence at Bhima Koregoan, various Dalit organisations called for a statewide *bandh*. In response, the police launched a combing operation – a large-scale search operation conducted without warrants – where they raided Dalit *bastis*, searched homes, rounded up young boys and men and humiliated women.[36] There were mass detentions in almost all Dalit neighbourhoods across Maharashtra and people fled their homes in fear. While 95 people were charged with attempted murder, over 3,000 people were illegally detained.

A Dalit activist we spoke to said that after a while it became impossible to keep track of all the arrests as they also completely wiped out the local leadership in various Dalit *bastis*. She told us that four years later, 'we still don't know how many people are in police custody and stuck there without access to lawyers'. The news media, she added, never bothered to report on this: 'Now it is just forgotten ... It sometimes feels like we have to be reduced to fighting for the lives of those in prison when the world outside is quietly and quickly being transformed into something more oppressive.'

Despite the overwhelming evidence of violence and a police-appointed fact-finding committee's statement that right-wing

---

34. Sukanya Shantha, 'A reporter saw the Bhima Koregaon violence coming. Now, he fears for his life.' *The Wire*, 18 September 2020.
35. Sukanya Shantha, 'Case against Hindutva leaders ignored, no justice in sight for Bhima Koregaon violence victims.' *The Wire*, 26 September 2020.
36. Sushmita, 'Hostile state machinery targets Dalits in Maharashtra.' *CJP*, 20 January 2018.

Hindu nationalist outfits had 'pre-planned' the Bhima Koregaon violence, a second FIR was filed with a contradictory narrative accusing the organisers of the Elgar Parishad conference.

Initially, only right-wing Hindu leaders Sambhaji Bhide and Milind Ekbote were investigated in the Bhima Koregaon violence. However, later, the police claimed that Naxals were responsible for the violence. One of the key witnesses of the violence, Pooja Sakat, a 19-year-old Dalit woman who had lost her house in the violence, was threatened to withdraw her statements against Bhide and Ekbote's men and was later found dead.

Sakat's family believes she was murdered because she was a critical eyewitness to the riots. While her death was initially ruled as suicide, after persistent protests, a case was finally registered and two people were arrested. However, the family allege that they continue to be threatened and targeted.

After the violence, the police did everything in their power to create fear, confusion and misinformation. They charged activists who had organised the Elgar Parishad as acting on behalf or of being members of the outlawed Communist Party of India (Maoists) and claimed that the Elgar Parishad was an anti-fascist front making inflammatory speeches and plotting to assassinate the prime minister. It is important to note that none of the accused was physically present at the site of violence and most were absent even at the Elgar Parishad.

Ignoring eyewitness testimonies, over the next three years the state built a case against 16 individuals (the BK16) on fabricated evidence. The original twosome accused of the violence, Sambhaji Bhide and Milind Ekbote – against whom there was substantial video evidence, social media evidence and eyewitnesses – continue to live with impunity while the state's noose around activists is beginning to tighten.

How does one make sense of the Elgar Parishad, the right-wing violence against Dalits at Bhima Koregaon and the arrest of the 16 activists?

What was essentially localised violence in the village of Bhima Koregaon was exploited to indict, arrest and club together various individuals under the 'Bhima Koregaon conspiracy case'. To understand these arrests, we need to ask who was arrested, for what reasons and why now? The answer keeps returning to the violence and plunder of Adivasi land, especially in Gadchiroli, to those who spoke against it, to the state's fear of new radical Dalit movements and the possibility of the wider left and anti-caste movements joining hands.

THEY FIRST CAME FOR THE LAWYERS

Surendra Gadling is the link that connects unabashed Dalit activism to the larger left. He defended countless people charged under terror laws labelled as Maoists or Naxalites. In his 25-year-long legal career, Gadling regularly challenged the state and was threatened in return. Legend has it that on his wedding day, he had to carry a copy of his anticipatory bail. One of the lawyers who apprenticed with him called him a 'street fighter, always up for a good fight'.

Almost all his cases were pro bono and everything he did was political, with anti-caste politics at the heart of his work. He represented those farthest from power – illegal killings, police violence and atrocities against Dalits and Adivasis. He fought for people victimised and wrongly booked in the Khairlanji's anti-Dalit violence, the Ramabai Nagar firing and the Thangjam Manorama murder case.[37] Gadling was a force to be reckoned with. People came from afar to hear him argue his points. He took on cases of political prisoners and defended G.N. Saibaba, journalist Prashant Rahi, Arun Ferreira, Dhanendra Bhurile, Vernon Gonsalves, Maruti Kurwatkarand and Sudhir Dhawale.

Long before his arrest, Suhas Bawache, the investigating officer who raided G.N. Saibaba's home, had threatened Gadling in the courtroom in front of his associates promising that 'once Saibaba is sent to prison, it will be the turn of Advocate Surendra Gadling'.[38]

A Dalit activist we spoke to also said that '[Bawache's] hand is all over their cases from Saibaba to Gadling'. Bawache, he alleged, was

---

37. Arijit Sen, 'Manipur's long wait for justice: remembering 1,528 cases and the murder of Thangjam Manorama.' *The Polis Project*, 22 November 2021.
38. This threat was also confirmed by one of Gadling's legal associates. Nilkantha Mandal, Sandeep Pandey and Kushagra Kumar, 'The man who used to get people acquitted in false cases has been implicated in one himself.' *Mainstream*, LIX (2), 26 December 2020.

also supervising the case without officially being part of the investigation. He was later transferred to Pune, where he lorded over the Bhima Koregaon arrests. Of all the officers who interrogated the arrested BK16, Bawache is known to be the most punitive, aggressive and abusive. In hindsight, it is clear that the state was already looking to arrest and silence lawyers and activists.

Initially, the police took no action against the second FIR that falsely accused the conveners of the Elgar Parishad of inciting violence at the behest of Maoists. However, in March 2018, without any inquiry or evidence, Surendra Gadling and Rona Wilson were charged with the offence of waging war against the state.

On 8 March 2018, the police requested a search warrant against Surendra Gadling, Sudhir Dhawale as well as Harshali Potdar, Rona Wilson, Sagar Gorkhe, Deepak Dhengle, Ramesh Gaichor, Jyoti Jagtap and Rupali Jadhav, which the judge rejected. The case was then quickly transferred to a different jurisdiction and, a month later in April, the warrants to search the residences were granted. In the simultaneous raids on all their homes – reminiscent of those in G.N. Saibaba's case – the police refused to show the warrant and took away everything: books, computers, family albums, booklets and movie CDs, including footage of right-wing violence at Bhima Koregaon from KKM members.

A plot to arrest and implicate Gadling and others was already brewing and spyware was used to plant false evidence in Rona Wilson's devices, which were subsequently seized by police in the raids.

CULPABLE HOMICIDE BY THE STATE

On 22 April 2018, as the dust settled on the illegal searches, an orchestrated massacre in the Gadchiroli district killed 40 people – 20 men and 20 women. The state called these 'encounters' the biggest success against armed resistance in India. News reports were triumphant and TV channels played video footage of security forces celebrating this success by dancing to popular Bollywood tunes.

Nagpur-based lawyer and Gadling's associate, Nihalsing Rathod, connected the aftermath of the Gadchiroli massacre with the events that culminated in the first round of arrests in the BK16 case. According to Rathod, various rights activists were part of the fact-finding report and visited the Gadchiroli district.[39] Surendra Gadling, Shoma Sen and Mahesh Raut supported these efforts. The findings included the gruesome nature of the killings and the discrepancies in the state's narrative. The report documented that most of the dead were children and called the massacre a 'culpable homicide by the state'.

Raut was arrested – along with Gadling, Dhawale, Wilson and Sen – the day before filing a petition with a local Adivasi leader in the Nagpur Bench of the Bombay High Court on 7 June.[40] Raut was under the state's radar since 2013 as he organised various local bodies to implement the Forest Rights Act, 2006.[41] On several occasions, he was detained and harassed by the police and, months before his arrest, his passport was confiscated.

The first round of BK16 arrests targeted Dalit and Bahujan activists and lawyers, who played an important role in defending the rights of Dalit and Adivasi communities, documenting the ongoing repression and questioning the state's violence directed towards grabbing Adivasi land for corporate plunder. The collusion between big business and the authoritarian state cannot be ignored. In June 2018, just before his arrest, Teltumbde argued that 'in Maharashtra, most people arrested as Maoists are Dalits and Adivasis. Their caste identity is compounded by the Maoist label, which renders them vulnerable.'[42]

With the second round of arrests, the police became more ambitious and cast a wider net: on 28 August 2018, they arrested Arun Ferreira, Sudha Bharadwaj, Varavara Rao and Vernon Gonsalves;

39. Coordination of Democratic Rights Organisations, Indian Association Peoples' Lawyers and Women Against Sexual Violence and State Repression, Encountering Resistance: State Policy for Development in Gadchiroli. People's Union for Democratic Rights, 2018.

40. Sukanya Shantha, 'Gadchiroli's 300 Gram Sabhas pass resolution in support of activist Mahesh Raut.' The Wire, 10 October 2018.

41. The Wire Staff, 'PM's rural development fellows come out in support of Mahesh Raut.' The Wire, 9 June 2018.

42. Teltumbde, 'Labelling Dalits and Adivasis as Maoists is an old state strategy for crushing dissent and criticism.'

on 14 April 2020, Anand Teltumbde and Gautam Navlakha; on 28 July 2020, Hany Babu; on 10 September 2020, KKM members Sagar Gorkhe, Ramesh Gaichor and the next day Jyoti Jagtap; finally on 8 October 2020, Father Stan Swamy was arrested in Ranchi.

Advocate Susan Abraham characterises the pattern of arrests as perfecting the model of repression.

What is the evidence against the BK16? The 17,000-page charge-sheet with over 200 witnesses is fraught with irregularities.

The evidence presented against the BK16 falls under two categories. First, information asserted without evidence; second, tampered evidence presented as a fact of complicity. A forensic report by Arsenal Consulting found that Rona Wilson's computer was compromised for over 22 months and that the attack was intended for two reasons: surveillance and planting incriminating documents using Netwire, a remote malware infrastructure. The attackers planted the ten main documents used as evidence in the chargesheet against Rona Wilson and other BK16 political prisoners. Arsenal called the attack 'one of the most serious cases of evidence tampering' ever encountered by their team. While the report does not state who is the perpetrator, it makes clear that 'the attack was deliberate and meticulously planned by a well-resourced agency.'[43]

The police can arrest anyone for being a Maoist, torture them and keep them tied up in multiple cases leaving them to languish in prison for four to five years, irrespective of what the courts decide. Most BK16 prisoners have been incarcerated since 2018.

THE CITY IS BURNING

From 23 February 2020, Northeast Delhi's Muslim communities were attacked by mobs, who destroyed property, attacked mosques and desecrated graveyards. Armed gangs first marked and then firebombed Muslim homes and businesses. They chanted *'Jai Shri Ram'*[44] as they set fire to a local mosque and planted

---

43.   Niha Masih and Joanna Slater, 'They were accused of plotting to overthrow the Modi government. The evidence was planted, a new report says.' *The Washington Post*, 12 November 2022.

44.   'Jai Shri Ram' literally means 'Victory to Lord Rama'. This invocation to the Hindu god Rama has turned into a hateful war call to incite attacks on Muslims.

Hindu nationalist flags on the minaret. The violence first broke out in Gokulpuri and from there, the slaughter quickly spread to several other areas including Seelampur, Shivpuri and Jafrabad and raged for four days before the violence finally ebbed.

Mobs roamed the streets, unchallenged by the police in the days following the riots: an inferno unleashed at the heart of the nation's capital. The perpetrators dumped bodies and severed limbs into open drains and bloated bodies were fished out of the gutter in the aftermath of the pogrom. An estimated 53 people died and many others, including children, remain missing. On the third day of violence, 7,500 emergency calls were made to the police control room, but no one arrived.[45]

Instead, the police worked with the rioters, aided and abetted them and sometimes even attacked the victims. Twenty-three-year-old Faizan and four other men were beaten repeatedly and forced to sing the national anthem. A gruesome video shows police officers surrounding the men, taunting, hitting and prodding them with sticks and instructing them to sing well as the men wither in pain. Later, he was illegally detained for over 36 hours, denied medical attention and died soon after. Police officers in uniform actively participated in violence and smashed CCTV cameras. Reporter Sagar wrote: 'Every time a police vehicle passed through the armed mob, the mob cheered them – some of them were casually chatting with the police with their sticks and lathis in hand. It seemed as if the armed mob was unafraid of the police.'[46] In his report from the streets of New Delhi, journalist Kaushal Shroff recorded members of a Hindu mob saying: '*Tension mat lo, sab apne hi log hain, Saare Hindu hi hai, aaj inn Mullo ki maiyya chod denge* (Don't take tension, all are your own people, all are Hindus, today we will fuck these *mullahs*' mothers).'[47] This hatred was reminiscent of the remarks made by Hindu mobs during the

45. Mukesh Singh Sengar, 'Cops got 7,500 calls for help on day 3 of Delhi violence: sources.' *NDTV*, 28 February 2020.

46. Sagar, 'Hindu supremacist mobs orchestrate violence against Muslims where BJP won in Delhi elections.' *The Caravan*, 25 February 2020.

47. Kaushal Shroff, 'Delhi violence: cops shouted "Jai Shri Ram" with armed Hindu mob, charged at Muslims.' *The Caravan*, 25 February 2020.

2002 Gujarat pogrom: '*Yeh andar ki baat hai, police hamaare saath hai* (It's an internal matter, the police are with us).'[48]

In a 1995 interview, senior police officer Vibhuti Narain Rai, speaking to human rights activist Teesta Setalvad, said: 'No riot can last for more than 24 hours without the consent of the state.'[49] In Delhi, the carnage was allowed to last for over four days and, in some places, mobs kept returning. After three years, many of the residents who fled remain homeless.

The violence began soon after local BJP politician Kapil Mishra posted a video threatening to take the matter into his own hands if the police did not clear the roads of protesters in three days.[50] Earlier, he led a large gathering calling to shoot the protesters. Several BJP leaders made divisive, hate-filled remarks against the people protesting at Shaheen Bagh in Northeast Delhi and incited violent attacks on protesters. BJP leader Parvesh Verma warned that those protesting in Shaheen Bagh 'will enter your homes, they will pick up your sisters and daughters and rape and kill them.'[51] In a Facebook live, self-styled Hindu leader Ragini Tiwari called on 'fellow Hindus' to 'come out. Die or kill'. She commanded her followers to *kaat do* (cut) the protestors. An eyewitness also saw her with people 'carrying big guns' and 'fire bullets in the air, after which the mob began losing control'.[52]

On 26 February 2020, Justice Muralidhar of the Delhi High Court questioned the Delhi Police about their refusal to file charges against hate speeches made by Anurag Thakur, Kapil Mishra, Parvesh Verma and Abhay Verma.[53] In open court, the

---

48.	The Polis Project, 'Manufacturing evidence: how the police are framing and arresting constitutional rights defenders in India.' *The Polis Project*, 21 January 2022.

49.	Teesta Setalvad in conversation with VN Rai, 'No riot can last for more than 24 hours unless the state wants it to continue.' *SabrangIndia*, February 1995.

50.	Human Rights Watch, 'Shoot the traitors.' *Human Rights Watch*, 16 June 2020.

51.	Scroll Staff, 'Shaheen Bagh protestors will "rape your sisters and daughters", says BJP MP on women-led protest.' *Scroll.in*, 20 January 2020.

52.	Aditya Menon and Aishwarya Iyer, '"Kaat do" said Ragini Tiwari, "eyewitness" saw her firing bullets.' *The Quint*, 30 June 2020.

53.	On 27 January 2020, at an election rally for a BJP candidate in Northwest Delhi, Anurag Thakur was filmed shouting the slogan '*Desh ke gaddaron ko*' multiple times, which was completed by the crowds that responded '*Goli maaro saalon ko*' (Shoot the traitors of the nation).

judge asked: 'You showed alacrity in lodging FIRs for arson; why aren't you showing the same for registering FIR for these speeches?'[54] Solicitor-General Tushar Mehta appearing on behalf of the state, claimed that the 'time wasn't conducive' to filing FIRs. Justice Muralidhar retorted: 'What is the appropriate time, Mr. Mehta? The city is burning.' Justice Muralidhar was transferred just hours after criticising the Delhi Police for inaction. The President of the Supreme Court Bar Association, Dushyant Dave, called the transfer 'absolutely malafide and punitive'. Justice Singh, the judge who replaced Justice Muralidhar, sided with the police and agreed that the situation was not immediately 'conducive' for registering police complaints against the men and women who incited violence.

When activist Harsh Mander filed a petition in the Supreme Court challenging the order and seeking action against the hate speech, the Solicitor-General arguing on behalf of the government accused Mander of inciting violence by making a speech about non-violence, peaceful protests and communal harmony and of being contemptuous of the Supreme Court. Lies became the truth and the truth no longer mattered. Fictions imagined by a petty sovereign became facts that required no evidence.

While being victims of the Northeast Delhi violence, Muslims were turned into perpetrators: according to Delhi Police, Muslims targeted their own communities, properties and people, killing fellow Muslims and burning their mosques to protest a discriminatory law directed towards their communities. In one instance, the police charged Haji Hasim Ali, the caretaker of the Madina Masjid in Shiv Vihar, for burning the mosque he administered. He was the complainant.

In many cases, the Delhi Police refused to register complaints from the Muslim community; in other cases, they lied and fabricated the complaints. For example, Delhi Police Sub-Inspector Harveer Singh Bhati from Okhla police station shot, point blank in front of three witnesses, 32-year-old Mohammad Furkan, who had stepped out to buy food for his children. In a statement given

---

54. Livelaw News Network, 'Delhi HC hearing in plea for probe into Delhi riots.' *LiveLaw.in*, 26 February 2020.

to *The Caravan*, Rukhsana Khatoon, Malka and Shehnaz, residents of Kardampuri, said that they saw Bhati murder Furkan.[55] Despite eyewitnesses, the chargesheet filed by the Delhi Police states that four Muslim men from the area killed him.

FIR 59

A few days later, on 6 March 2020, the Delhi Police registered the notorious FIR No. 59/2020 (FIR 59 or the Delhi riots conspiracy case), which has since become an expanding sinkhole of charges, allegations, manufactured evidence and arrests. If the BK16 case made dissenting opinions against the state a crime, through FIR 59, the Delhi conspiracy charges successfully equated democratic protests with provocation. The police alleged that the anti-CAA protests created a communally charged atmosphere that led to the violence in February. The 'riots' were thus simply a retaliation to the protests.

Initially, student leader Umar Khalid was named as the prime accused along with Danish, a resident of Northeast Delhi; they were charged with 'rioting, using deadly weapons, unlawful assembly and criminal conspiracy' and later charged under the UAPA. Danish was arrested in the case on 9 March 2020 and released four days later. Umar Khalid was detained six months later, on 13 September, and, at the time of writing, is still in prison unable to secure bail.

By the end of the year, 18 others were arrested under FIR 59 – Faizan Khan, Sharjeel Imam, Natasha Narwal, Devangana Kalita, Ishrat Jahan, Gulfisha Fatima, Meeran Haider, Safoora Zargar, Asif Iqbal Tanha, Taahir Hussain, Mohd Parvez Ahmed, Mohd Illyas, Khalid Saifi, Shahdab Ahmed, Tasleem Ahmed, Saleem Malik, Mohd Saleem Khan and Athar Khan. Safoora Zargar was three months pregnant at the time of her arrest. Sharjeel Imam, arrested long before the Delhi violence on 28 January, was also implicated in the conspiracy with sedition charges. 16 of the 19 charged are Muslim – almost three years later, the police continue to use FIR 59 to detain, surveil and harass Muslim students and activists.

---

55.   Sumedha Mittal and Amir Malik, 'Three eyewitnesses accuse Delhi police official of murder during Delhi violence.' *The Caravan*, 12 February 2021.

Activist and local leader Meeran Haider's lawyer Naved calls FIR 59 'an innovation in criminal law' and 'a blank cheque that can be encashed any time'.[56]

This strategy of staggered arrests created an atmosphere of fear and imminent and ever-present precarity, where anyone who participated in the protests could be called in. Anyone could be arrested at any time, not just for organising the protest but even for supporting the cause.

Six months after the charges were first filed, on 16 September, the Delhi Police brought to the courtroom a 17,000-page chargesheet in a large steel trunk. In the case, however, there is no substantive evidence except for the testimony of an informer. The chargesheet relies on a pamphlet written by student activist Sharjeel Imam against CAA; screenshots of alleged WhatsApp messages exchanged between various students and activists; their Facebook posts. Many messages cited as evidence of conspiracy are protest announcements readily available in the public domain.

In the aftermath of the violence, many young people, especially Muslim boys from violence-hit neighbourhoods, were rounded up, interrogated and threatened. Many people had been allegedly coerced into accusing civil rights activists of instigating the

---

56.   Seemi Pasha, 'The Delhi violence FIRs are like blank cheques, to be encashed by the police any time.' *The Wire*, 30 April 2020.

February attacks, particularly those connected to the anti-CAA protests. Two witnesses have admitted to testifying under duress, one stating that he was forced to falsely implicate Umar Khalid.[57]

The police argued that popular protests, gatherings and marches are proof of a conspiracy to incite violence. *Chakka jams* (road blockades); sit-in protests like Shaheen Bagh; demonstrations held at Jantar Mantar, the iconic protest venue in Central Delhi; or marches that started from Jamia Millia Islamia University were all labelled as events used to instigate violence and riots while anti-CAA protest organisers were accused of acting in furtherance of their common conspiracy.

The FIR 59 turned protestors into rioters and the act of gathering, guaranteed under the Indian Constitution, into an offence. The chargesheet is filled with allegations of inflammatory speeches, instigating women to protest and even an absurd offence of stockpiling various articles. The proof of organising a protest quickly became an allegation of inciting violence, committing a terrorist act or of a conspiracy to commit a terrorist act. The FIR does not talk about any actual crime, instead, it is a patchwork of conspiracy theories that have no basis in law.

NO EVIDENCE, ONLY CONSPIRACY

The voluminous chargesheet brought another set of troubles. The police refused to give the accused and their lawyers photocopies of the chargesheet according to the law. Booked under terror laws, denied bail and detained indefinitely without trial, those accused have also been denied the right to properly defend themself. One of the lawyers we interviewed commented:

[The Delhi Police] are making everything difficult. They don't follow the rules and laws or care for orders by the Court. Even after the Court specifically directed them to give the chargesheet, they still haven't. The Delhi Police have always enjoyed immense

---

57. The Wire Staff, 'Citing instance of "witness" coercion, Umar Khalid accuses police of framing him in riots case.' *The Wire*, 2 September 2020.

power, but this is the first time we encounter this *nautanki*, this stubborn refusal to share the physical copy of a chargesheet.[58]

The chargesheets also arrived heavily redacted and the contents of key statements were incomprehensible. While UAPA provisions allow for redaction, in this case the extent of redaction made it impossible for the accused to understand the entirety of the case against them. The unbridled and unprincipled redaction of witness statements further crippled the ability of the accused to defend themselves, reducing the bail hearing to a charade. The lawyer added: 'It's like you are blindfolded, your hands are tied and you are dropped into a boxing ring. You don't know where the punches are coming from or who is attacking you, but you are expected to fight.'

मैं एक xxxxxxx चलाता हूँ । मैं xxxxxxxxx का स्टूडेंट हूँ । मेरा आजमी (Alumini Association of Jamia Milia Islamia) मे आना जाना था । मैं शफ़ाउल रहमान, अरीब हसन और दानिश को जानता था । लॉकडाउन शुरू होने के बाद अरीब ने मुझसे बोला "मुझे खाली xxxxxxxx चाहिए" । मैंने नहीं दिए । अरीब मेरे ऊपर दबाव बनाता रहा । अप्रैल के फ़र्स्ट वीक मे मैंने अपने दोस्त xxxxxxx से बात करी । मैंने अपने xxxxx की xxxxxx और xxxxxxxxxx अरीब को दी थी । अरीब ने xxxxxxxxxxxx (दोनों) मुझे शाम को वापिस कर दी ।
मुझे स्पेशल सेल से एक दिन फोन आया । मुझे स्पेशल सेल ने मुझे दो xxxxx दिखाये । एक मुसाब की xxxxxxxxx का था । दूसरा मेरी xxxxxxxxx का था । मुसाब की xxxxxx का xxxxxxxxxx रुपए का था । मेरी xxxxxxx का xxxxxxxxxxxxxxx रुपए का था । इन xxxxxxx से मेरा कोई लेना देना नहीं है । मैंने ये xxxxxxx दबाव मे दिए थे । अरीब ने बताया था की xxxxxx उसे आजमी का पैसा एडजस्ट करने के लिए चाहिए ।
Xxxxxxxxx पर मेरी राइटिंग या साइन नहीं है ।

The chargesheet does not contain any evidence that places any of the arrested at the crime scene or committing an offence. In the CCTV footage presented as evidence they are either not visible or,

---

58.   Many lawyers defending those arrested after the Delhi violence had to turn their clients down because they did not have the technical infrastructure to deal with the massive FIRs shared through pen drives and pdfs.

if they are, it does not show 'them carrying out violent criminal acts or inciting violence'.[59]

In June 2021, Pinjra Tod activists Natasha Narwal and Devangana Kalita and Jamia student Asif Iqbal Tanha were released. While granting bail, the Session Court observed that 'in an anxiety to suppress dissent, the state has blurred the line between the right to protest and terrorist activity' and called it a 'sad day for democracy'.[60]

The Court explicitly ruled on the lack of evidence of their crime. In Narwal's case, the judge noted that 'videos show her being a part of unlawful assembly but do not show the accused indulging or inciting the violence'. While granting bail to Devangana Kalita, the Court noted that her presence is seen in peaceful agitation, a fundamental right guaranteed under Article 19 of the Constitution, and that the police 'failed to produce any material that she in her speech instigated women of a particular community or gave hatred speech due to which the precious life of a young man has been sacrificed and property damaged'. In Tanha's bail, the judge noted the absence of proof to substantiate the allegation that the anti-CAA protests were part of a larger conspiracy to cause terror. The judge noted that the chargesheet's 'use of alarming and hyperbolic verbiage will not convince us otherwise' and concluded that charges were based on 'inferences drawn by the prosecuting agency and not upon factual allegations'.

Despite the Court's acknowledgement of these grave mistakes, others arrested under the Delhi conspiracy case continue to languish in prison. The stringent conditions of bail incentivise the investigating agencies to invoke the UAPA even if there is insubstantial evidence, only to ensure long periods of undertrial custody.

On the day of their release, standing at the prison gate, Natasha, Asif and Devangana raised their fists in the air and yelled: '*Dum hai kitna daman mein tere, dekh liya hai, dekhenge. Jagah hai kitni*

---

59. Order dated 17 November 2020, *State* v. *Ajay*, Bail Application No. 2058/2020, Additional Sessions Judge, Karkardooma District Court, Delhi.
60. Press Trust of India, 'Delhi riots: HC asks police to respond to bail plea of student activist in larger conspiracy case.' *The Indian Express*, 11 May 2022. The following quotes are also taken from the same article.

jail mein tere, dekh liya hai, dekhenge (How much oppression can you unleash? We have seen it, we shall see. How much space do your prisons have? We have seen them, we shall see).'

Their bail remains the exception.

WHEN THE PETITIONER IS THE CRIMINAL

India has long been a country where thousands can be incarcerated for years without being convicted in a court of law, but things took a turn for the worse when the country's highest constitutional court criminalised the very act of approaching the courts to seek justice.

Zakia Jafri's husband, former minister Ehsan Jafri, was hacked and burned alive. He was one of the 68 people killed inside the gated Gulbarg Society, in the city of Ahmedabad a day after the 2002 Godhra violence in Gujarat. Helped by rights activist Teesta Setalvad, 85-year-old Zakia has been fighting for justice since 2006, when she filed a petition asking why the police had not registered the case against Prime Minister Modi (the then chief minister of Gujarat) and others in connection with the violence.

After 16 years, on 24 June 2022, Justice Khanwilkar of the Supreme Court dismissed her plea calling it 'devoid of merits' and accused Zakia of keeping the pot boiling by filing legal petitions for ulterior design. He chastised her and Teesta Setalvad for having the 'audacity to question the integrity of every functionary involved in the process'.[61]

The judgment made it clear that rather than adjudicating the case, Justice Khanwilkar indulged in what can only be called defamation, treating both women as figures to be ridiculed. In contrast, he commended the state for their indefatigable work and claimed they had come out with flying colours. Calumny is not what one expects from the highest constitutional court, yet here we are.

The same Supreme Court in 2004 commenting on the case took a different position and said:

---

61. Satish Jha, 'SC order on Zakia Jafri's appeal "illegal, unconstitutional and violates every tenet of law". *CJP*, 8 July 2022.

The modern-day 'Neros' were looking elsewhere when … innocent children and helpless women were burning and were probably deliberating how the perpetrators of the crime can be saved or protected. Law and justice become flies in the hands of these wanton boys … One gets a feeling that the justice … was being taken for a ride and allowed to be abused, misused, and mutilated by subterfuge. The investigation appears to be per-functory and anything but impartial without any definite object of finding out the truth and bringing to book those who were responsible for the crime.[62]

It is unbecoming of a constitutional bench to perform such obeisance, especially towards agencies accused of orchestrating pogroms and, later, obstructing justice.

The day after the judgment, on 25 June 2022, Teesta Setalvad and former senior police officer R.B. Sreekumar, who had played an essential role in exposing facts about the Gujarat pogrom, were arrested by the Gujarat Police, citing the Supreme Court judgment as the basis of the arrests.

A few days later, Justice Khanwilkar presided over another case involving state violence: the extrajudicial encounter killings during the Gompad massacre of Adivasis in Chhattisgarh. The fact that the massacre happened and that 16 Adivasis – including women, children and the elderly – were murdered in Chhattisgarh in 2009 is not disputed. Every Adivasi petitioner in the case named and identified the police officials who perpetrated the massacre.[63] However, upon hearing the plea, the Court ruled that it found no evidence against the police and accused rights activist Himanshu Kumar, who filed the petition, 'to Help Naxalites'. Justice Khan-wilkar dismissed the petition and imposed a fine of Rs. 500,000 on Kumar. He arrived at this conclusion without ordering an investi-gation: dead bodies were no longer proof of death. The judge also granted investigative agencies vast powers to file a case of criminal conspiracy against Kumar.

---

62.   V. Venkatesan, 'A judicial stricture.' *Frontline Magazine*, 6 May 2004.
63.   Writ Petition No. 103 of 2009 Himanshu Kumar And Others Versus State Of Chhattisgarh And Others.

In a case of indisputable conflict of interest, the senior police officer in charge of Chhattisgarh during the massacre – the accused himself – was now the head of the investigative agency given the power to prosecute Kumar. The judge relied on the submission of the perpetrator to acquit him of any liability.

Kumar refused to pay the fine, saying he had done nothing wrong and responded: 'Seeking justice is not a crime in this country ... As long as the matter has not been investigated by any agency appointed or monitored by the Supreme Court, how can it be described as false?'[64]

The Court could have dismissed the petition without going into the merits of both cases. Yet, it chose to penalise the petitioners without evidence, declaring that they acted maliciously and intentionally abused the law. By accepting the state's version of the events prima facie, the Court tacitly endorsed the argument made by the state against Kumar that the cases filed against the security forces were done to help the Naxalites.

Activist Kavita Krishnan called the judgment the 'Last rites of India's Constitution'[65] and Justice A.P. Shah called the decision shocking. The Court had not just crossed the line, it bulldozed what Ambedkar called the 'heart and soul of the Constitution', Article 32, which guarantees the right to approach the Supreme Court to enforce rights.

This is an unprecedented moment where unsubstantiated pernicious remarks made by the Supreme Court could become the basis for persecuting those approaching the courts. Kumar concluded: 'This means all the human rights activists' who come to the Supreme Court to seek justice 'are criminals and can be jailed'.

---

64. Press Trust of India, 'Seeking justice is no crime, won't pay fine imposed by Supreme Court, says activist.' *The Print*, 19 July 2022.
65. Kavita Krishnan statement on Twitter, 14 July 2022.

3

The Lies Factory

In December 2022, Sub-Divisional Police Officer Ganesh More declared under oath: 'I did not come across any information or material to show that the incident of riots which took place on 1st January 2018, was a result of holding of Elgar Parishad on 31st December 2017 at Shaniwar Wada, Pune.'[1] He made his deposition in front of a two-member judicial commission enquiring on the claims made by the Pune Police and later by the NIA against the BK16. More, now retired, was one of the main investigating officers in the case. This was the first time a public official had openly admitted that there was no actual evidence to connect the statements made during the Elgar Parishad meeting with the violence that took place at the Bhima Koregaon commemoration the following day. In other words, there is no reason grounded in facts that justifies that the BK16 are in jail.

As India prides itself on being the largest democracy in the world, a revelation of this scale should have shaken the very foundations of the government. The news, however, caused almost no reaction and the outrage for the admission – felt only in relatively small circles – died out quickly. Unperturbed, Narendra Modi continues in his ethno-nationalist makeover of the country and More's declaration to date proved to be of no consequence.

In a statement of disarming candour, retired Major General Rajan Kochhar said that 'It would be premature right now to equate a civil society in the same category as terror groups and insurgents and by any stretch of imagination ask the Police to take them now.'[2] We should all be alarmed by Kochhar's argument that

1.   Sukanya Shantha, 'Top investigating officer admits Elgar Parishad event "had no role" in Bhima Koregaon Violence.' *The Wire*, 27 December 2022.
2.   Rajan Kochhar, 'Civil society heading to the danger of a new frontier; are we prepared?' *India Times*, 7 February 2022.

the equation between civil society and terror groups is only 'premature' now: not inconceivable, but rather something that sooner or later may become a reality.

This statement is not, however, the isolated musing of an ultra-conservative retired army officer. Instead, it follows quite closely the path marked by no less than the National Security Advisor of India, Ajit Doval.

Doval, in November 2021, in an address to the probationary officers at the Sardar Vallabhbhai Patel National Police Academy in Hyderabad declared: 'People are most important. The new frontiers of war – what we call the fourth-generation warfare – is the civil society.'[3] As military wars are too uncertain and costly or no longer effective, civil society is the new battleground as it 'can be subverted, divided, and can be manipulated, to hurt the interest of the nation'.

Fourth-generation warfare is defined as a kind of conflict where the lines between war and politics, civilians and combatants blur and where non-state actors are no longer proxies, but the main threat to the very existence of a country. In Doval's speech, the language of war openly enters the public domain and defines the terms of the debate about political opposition and critical dissent. Civil society – which is meant to be the very soul of a functioning democracy – thus turns into a potential enemy of the state, into a threatening entity ready to hurt its interests, into a menace that needs to be eradicated.

As words make worlds, the gap between intentions and deeds shrinks, devoiding the very notion of accountability. The state is no longer culpable of killing dissent; it is, on the contrary, applauded for giving utmost priority to national security and to the incolumity of the country. As we mentioned in the Introduction, the Supreme Court in 2016 refused to admit a PIL that called for greater scrutiny on the use of public funding and the activities of India's intelligence agencies. This decision sanctioned the fact that India is the only democracy in the world where intelligence agencies – whose task is supposedly the preservation of national

---

3. Pia Krishnankutty, 'Civil society is new frontier of war, can be subverted to harm nation, Ajit Doval says.' *The Print*, 13 November 2021.

security, hence something of public interest – are not accountable to anyone, neither to the Parliament nor to the people, de facto allowing them to exist beyond the pale and thus to act with total impunity.

In this climate, it is no longer needed to commit a crime to be treated like a criminal. The words used by Justice M.R. Shah – a member of the special two-judges bench convened early morning on a Saturday in October 2022 to re-examine the acquittal of Saibaba and five others and stay a release order issued less than 24 hours earlier – are a monument to this new India. With no fear of retribution, he said on record that for terrorist and Maoist activities, 'the brain is more dangerous. Direct involvement is not necessary.'

The consequences of words of this kind need to be carefully analysed. The enormity of this statement undermines the Indian justice system from its foundations, it removes the evidence of a crime from the equation and it allows for the construction of guilt to be entirely based on suspicion, speculation and, basically, antipathy. Intellectual, religious, caste, political dislike thus becomes a sufficient reason to frame opponents or dissenters as criminals and lock them up in jail for years on end.

Again, Justice M.R. Shah's declaration is neither an isolated voice nor is it an exception. In the same month, in fact only three days later, on 18 October 2022, an argument of the same tenure was presented before and accepted by the Delhi High Court.

Umar Khalid had appealed for bail in the case filed against him under the infamous FIR 59 where he was charged under various sections of the IPC, 1980, including rioting (Sections 147 and 148), murder (302) and unlawful assembly (149). He was also charged under the UAPA for unlawful and terrorist activities as well as for conspiracy; and under the Arms Act, 1959, for the use of weapons. Advocate Trideep Pais, Umar Khalid's legal counsel, argued that there was no evidence to substantiate the charges against his client. The bench of the Delhi High Court, however, rejected the plea stating that there was a legitimate prima facie case for the prosecution.

It is important to note that the reason for denying bail is that the judges found a speech that Umar Khalid gave during the anti-CAA protests 'hateful, inciteful, offensive & obnoxious'. To this, trying to bring back the discussion on legal grounds rather than on personal taste, Advocate Pais replied: 'We are here for conspiracy to commit terror on the basis of this speech. It is one thing for your lordships to find the speech obnoxious and ridiculous, but quite another for the UAPA to be levied on this basis.'[4]

In a later hearing of the case, Justices Siddharth Mridul and Rajnesh Bhatnagar stated that under the UAPA, 'it is not just the intent to threaten the unity and integrity but the likelihood to threaten the unity and integrity'[5] of the nation that is at stake. It is therefore not necessary to have evidence that a threatening act has been committed or intended, it is sufficient to venture in the abstract realm of suspicions, of maybes and perhaps to lock someone up.

As far as we know today – with a confirmation from the stunning declaration of Ganesh More – the BK16, Umar Khalid and many other political prisoners have been arrested and kept in jail based on the likelihood that they may have meant something harmful, a likelihood that has no solid anchor whatsoever in reality.

In proceedings that Advocate Pais defined more apt as a script of the TV series *Family Man* than deemed worthy of a courtroom, Justices Mridul and Bhatnagar added:

The call to revolution may affect many beyond those who were visibly present, which is why this court finds it apt to mention Robespierre, who was at the vanguard of the French revolution. This court is of the view that possibly, if the appellant had referred to Maximilien Robespierre for what he meant by revolution, he must have also known what revolution meant for our freedom fighter & first prime minister. The very fact that Pandit Jawaharlal Nehru believed that democracy has made revolution superfluous after independence and how it meant the complete opposite of a bloodless change. Revolution by itself isn't always bloodless, which is why it is contradistinctly used with the prefix

---

4. Tishya Saran, 'Umar Khalid's speech hateful & inciteful': Delhi High Court during oral exchange in plea challenging refusal of bail.' *LawBeat*, 22 April 2022.
5. Compiled from the live Twitter feed of LiveLaw on 18 October 2022.

– a 'bloodless' revolution. So, when we use the expression 'revolution,' it is not necessarily bloodless.[6]

As able spin doctors who mystify reality, Justices Mridul and Bhatnagar produced a spectacular conflagration of times and history to make Umar Khalid guilty of inciting violence. The supposed incriminating 'call to revolution' refers to the use of the expression *Inquilab Zindabad* (long live the revolution) that has been a core feature of democratic struggle in India even before its inception as an independent nation state. The slogan, coined by Urdu poet and freedom fighter Maulana Hasrat Mohani in 1921, was then made popular by Bhagat Singh, became a unifying cry of the Indian independence movement and has been part of the Indian rights movements since.

As it is sadly typical, authoritarianism and historical revisionism go hand in hand. In India, all state apparatuses have put together a concerted effort to rewrite Indian history; an effort that begins with the silencing of all those who reclaim a factual anchoring to the complex history of the country. And so, eradicated from its historical meaning and taken out of context, *Inquilab Zindabad* becomes an incitement to violence rather than an expression of critical citizenship.

Authoritarian regimes distort language and kill ideas, arguments, institutions and dissenting voices – all in the name of ideology masquerading as history, reality and truth. Lies are now proof of a non-existent crime even when they are countered and revealed as such. It is as if truth is no longer permissible evidence before the law.

For instance, in February 2021, journalist Ismat Ara interviewed BJP's Kapil Mishra about his hate speech and role in the Delhi pogrom that ensued. Mishra, with absolute confidence, initially denied being there and demanded proof. However, when Ara confronted him with the video, he quickly changed his tone and said he was proud of what he had done. He then defended the *goli maaron saalon ko* slogan – a chant that encourages the killing of traitors

---

6. Ibid.

of the country – after denying its existence and proclaimed: 'If it happens like that again, I will do that again.'

The video of his lies, obfuscation and final confession of inciting violence went viral, but Kapil Mishra remains free. If anything, playing fast and loose with truth further strengthened his appeal. Amit Malviya, the BJP's national Information and Technology Cell in-charge, did more than just incite violence; he became the merchant of disinformation whose lies eventually led to the arrest of Umar Khalid.

In March 2020, Malviya tweeted a doctored video showing student leader and activist Umar Khalid asking Muslims to 'come out on streets in huge numbers when Trump arrives in India.' He falsely claimed that Khalid's speech led to the Delhi pogrom that killed over 53 people (mostly Muslim). The edited video was quickly broadcast and repeatedly played on Republic TV, News18, Zee News and Times Now – all media outlets that are close allies of the current dispensation. Other media platforms like *The Times of India*, *Hindustan Times* and *India Today* also widely shared this duplicitous claim.

Taking the cue from BJP leadership, the Delhi Police claimed that Khalid's speech instigated the violence. While TV anchors took on the role of judge and jury and conducted media trials based on lies, the Delhi Police threatened and coerced an acquaintance to give a false confession against Khalid.

During Khalid's bail plea in August 2021, his lawyer Trideep Pais presented evidence that Republic TV and News18 news channels used the footage doctored by BJP's Amit Malviya. He further argued that none of the channels possessed the raw footage of the speech and never fact-checked the altered video shared by Malviya. Pais also played the entire speech in court and pointed out that nothing in Khalid's speech was 'seditious or instigated violence'.[7]

Despite overwhelming procedural impropriety, lack of evidence and a fictitious chargesheet, Khalid has been incarcerated for over three years. India now has a growing number of political prisoners, all incarcerated with false or fabricated evidence. The institu-

---

7.   The Wire Staff, 'Delhi riots conspiracy case "cooked up", was "framed by media": Umar Khalid.' *The Wire*, 23 August 2021.

tional murder of Father Stan Swamy is an egregious example of the cruelty of the state.

The 84-year-old Jesuit priest, one of the BK16, was the oldest person arrested on terror charges. He was incarcerated without evidence during the pandemic, denied care and medical treatment and refused bail despite deteriorating health. In prison, he was denied a straw to drink water as he struggled with Parkinson's disease. Despite these glaring actions of neglect, cruelty and inhumane treatment the government claimed it had acted within the due process of law.

As Father Stan Swamy's health deteriorated rapidly, his medical bail – the final attempt to save his life – was vehemently opposed by the NIA, claiming that there was no 'conclusive proof' that he was ill.[8] The Court was persuaded to deny mercy to a man fighting for his life on the grounds of concocted lies.

Justice S.S. Shinde of the Bombay High Court, one of the judges who consistently denied Father Stan bail, was forced to retract the statements he made praising him after his death. This came after the NIA raised objections. In profound irony, the agency claimed that 'there is a negative perception being created against the NIA.' However, what is crucial here is the NIA's demand to erase even the modicum of empathy and truth that judges could conjure from the official legal record.

Lies work in multiple ways – and here it was rewriting history and reality before us.

Almost 18 months after Father Stan Swamy's death, in December 2022, forensic company Arsenal Consulting found evidence that multiple 'incriminating files' were planted on his computer by a hacker, including fabricated letters between Father Stan and the leader of the Maoist insurgency.[9] The report states that 'Swamy was the target of an extensive malware campaign for nearly five years … right up until police seized his device in June 2019.'[10]

---

8.   Times of India, 'How Stan Swamy's long struggle for bail ended in tragedy.' *The Times of India*, 5 July 2021.
9.   Niha Masih, 'Hackers planted evidence on computer of jailed Indian priest, report says.' *The Washington Post*, 13 December 2022.
10. Ibid.

The hacker read and copied as many as 24,000 files on Father Stan's device and planted over 50 files between July 2017 and June 2019.[11] The Arsenal report found that hours before Swamy's computer was seized by the police, an extensive 'cleanup' of the hack was performed, signalling collusion between the hacker and the investigating agencies. Arsenal's president Mark Spencer called the scale of the attack against Father Stan 'truly unprecedented'.

The planted documents were the basis for his arrest and continue to be used as evidence against other BK16 prisoners. Senior Advocate Mihir Desai in a press conference said that Father Stan's death sentence was finalised on the day he was arrested.[12]

Father Stan had consistently denied all the charges against him and called the evidence against him fabricated. In response, the NIA called the allegations of fabricating evidence and Father Stan's declaration of his innocence an 'endeavour to confuse truth with falsehood and to create a mist around the evidence and reality'.[13]

Since these startling revelations, nothing has changed. The NIA has not denied the reports, the courts remain silent despite evidence of state criminality and activists and lawyers continue the fight to clear Father Stan Swamy's name.

In *Goebbels: A Biography*, German historian Peter Longerich writes about Hitler's propaganda minister, using over 30,000 pages of Goebbels' diary entries. The entries are chilling. For example, Longerich reproduces a passage where Goebbels fabricates an assassination attempt against himself and claims that a plot was hatched to kill him. *Der Angriff*, the Nazi party newspaper, covered this widely on its front pages. Yet, even after evidence emerged that Goebbels had faked the assassination attempt, the news was never retracted. On the contrary, Goebbels wrote in his diary that the 'assassination attempt' was 'a genuine threat'.[14] Longerich adds that

---

11.   Ibid.
12.   SabrangIndia, 'The death of Fr. Stan Swamy was finalised the day he was arrested: Senior Advocate Mihir Desai.' *SabrangIndia*, 26 December 2022.
13.   Press Trust of India, 'Probe agency opposes activist Stan Swamy's bail plea, calls him Maoist.' *NDTV*, 17 June 2021.
14.   Peter Longerich, *Goebbels: A Biography*. Random House, 2015, p. 282.

'having acted out a charade for public consumption, he [Goebbels] then recorded it as a fact in his diary'.[15]

Goebbels' invention of reality and his later assertion that this was indeed the truth is a crucially infamous precedent to what we are witnessing in India today – he did not see the contradiction between fact and fiction, truth and propaganda. Goebbels' deception and his charade, therefore, do not feel like history – they are the past reproducing itself.

---

15.   Ibid.

4

A Community in Resistance

In the 1920s and 1930s in Italy, the fascist regime used as a common policing practice the *confino di polizia* or *confino* (police confinement, forced exile), a pre-emptive measure to isolate dissidents and political opponents from civil society. Originating from an 1863 monarchical law, the fascist version of the decree made it easy to ban from political life all those who were considered by the regime a threat to national unity and public order. There was no need for trial and it was enough to receive a private police complaint to implement the measure. Dissidents were picked up and sent to remote islands or small mountain villages for years on end, they were kept under strict police surveillance and were legally equated to criminals. Many prominent anti-fascist Italian intellectuals – as well as sexual minorities – were deemed dangerous for public safety and cut off physically, emotionally and socially from their communities.[1]

What seems a feature of a different time in history is in fact prominently present in contemporary political life, where democratic participation is fading and spaces of free expression and dissent are shrinking across the globe. While the very definition of political prisoner may sound outdated, jail is a stark reality for many dissidents, intellectuals and activists who are incarcerated on fabricated charges and kept as undertrials in a complete denial of most basic rights for months and years.

In his autobiographical novel *Christ Stopped at Eboli*, Italian anti-fascist intellectual Carlo Levi recalled his own experience as a political prisoner in *confino*. In the book there is an episode that keeps coming back to mind as symbolic of the unjustified cruelty

---

1. Agnese Bentivogli, 'Una via di mezzo tra esilio e prigionia: il confino, l'arma di repressione silenziosa del regime fascista.' *Parentesi Storiche*, 18 October 2018.

exercised by the state against political prisoners, the role that small gestures play in preserving humanity and the undeterred power of solidarity. There were other political prisoners in *confino* along with Levi in the small village of Grassano in Southern Italy, two of them were young men of very limited economic means. The state would not provide for the prisoners so the two men started to take turns cooking the daily meal for each other to make things financially more manageable. By law, prisoners were not allowed to speak to each other or socialise – if they were caught interacting, they would be arrested and sent to jail – so the two young men had to make sure they would not get caught. They would wait until the time of the siesta when everyone was asleep and sneakily leave a plate of pasta on a bench in the square for the other.

The narration of episodes of camaraderie and solidarity, such as the one that Levi recalled, was a constant element in the conversations with family members of Indian political prisoners. It is hardly ever the case that, with surveillance and abuses of power, the state succeeds in its intent to deplete people of their humanity: small gestures of mutual care keep it alive, both inside and outside prison. bell hooks reminds us that building a community requires vigilant awareness and that '[t]alking together is one way to make community'.[2]

In a context where the narrative is split between enemies and victims, the point is to move away from the reification of power dynamics where a self-appointed spokesperson gives voice to those who supposedly do not have one of their own. Talking together implies the reclamation of political agency and the ethical construction of a shared political discourse. The diverse community that gravitates around Indian political prisoners is mostly aggregated around the defence of equal citizenship and the upholding of basic constitutional values. Therefore, the necessity of talking together to produce a counternarrative – a necessity that is very much at the core of this book – comes as an urgency to both oppose logics of victimisation and respond to the poisonous tones of the Indian government and its lackeys.

---

2.   bell hooks, *All about Love: New Visions*. Harper Perennial, 2001, p. 133.

The public discourse around political prisoners in India is highly polarised and the so-called *godi* media[3] play a major role in the demonisation of government's opponents through the elaboration of a vocabulary that banks on people's fears and innermost irrational feelings. Definitions such as terrorists, Urban Naxals, anti-nationals contribute to the dehumanisation of individuals whose life is devoted to the defence of the rights of the most vulnerable sections of society even when this means to collide in a frontal clash with the brutality of the state apparatuses. Indian political prisoners are students, public intellectuals, lawyers, artists, human rights defenders, activists who are rooted in underprivileged communities that resist the abuses, the oppression and the impunity with which the state and its institutions utterly disregard the Constitution. The vulgar language used by the media to define dissidents and dissenters removes them from the social fabric that makes them who they are and singles them out as made up threats to the state and to society at large.

While weaving together these fragments of intimate narrations to fully understand the broader picture, a myriad of details started to emerge with a common thread of kindness, care, sense of justice, hope, commitment, sacrifice as well as love and dedication. This is why Koel, the daughter of Shoma Sen, was almost piqued by the fact that we felt it would be important to construct a more humanising picture of individuals who have been extracted away from their contexts and turned into political icons: 'How would people even remotely doubt that they [the political prisoners] are the most human of human beings? They have sacrificed all they have and are in jail for their ideas, how can anyone doubt their humanity?'

For Devangana Kalita this is a difficult new reality to negotiate. Besides having to digest the awfulness that her detractors throw at her, she feels deeply uncomfortable for the way friendly voices have eulogised and singled out their role. It is important, she said,

---

3. *Godi* media is the term that in India has come to define loudmouthed media outlets that run as de facto state propaganda machines by publishing whatever the government asks them to and by contributing to the hate-mongering communal undertones that characterise the current political dispensation. *Godi* in Hindi means 'lap' and the expression is a word play with Modi's name that alludes to Indian media behaving as the prime minister's lap dog.

to demystify this narrative and make people understand that this is not about individual heroism, but that the courage and strength come from the community and from the fight itself. For Devangana, like for many others, this is not about themselves – it is about the struggle.

On 15 January 2021, when he completed a hundred days in jail, Father Stan Swamy wrote:

First of all, I deeply appreciate the overwhelming solidarity expressed by many during these past 100 days behind the bars. At times, news of such solidarity has given me immense strength and courage especially when the only thing certain in prison is uncertainty. Life here is on a day-to-day basis. Another strength during these past hundred days, has been in observing the plight of the undertrials. A majority of them come from economically & socially weaker communities. Many of such poor undertrials don't know what charges have been put on them, have not seen their charge sheet and just remain in prison for years without any legal or other assistance. Overall, almost all undertrials are compelled to live to a bare minimum, whether rich or poor. This brings in a sense of brotherhood & communitarianism where reaching out to each other is possible even in this adversity. On the other hand, we sixteen co-accused have not been able to meet each other, as we are lodged in different jails or different 'circles' within the same jail. But we will still sing in chorus. *A caged bird can still sing.*[4]

This profound sense of humanity, these small gestures of mutual care, these droplets of hope have been at the centre of our encounters with the families of political prisoners and with former political prisoners themselves. There has hardly been any conversation that has not started with a long discussion on the status of other prisoners and their families and immediate communities. As the news of our meetings went around, people started asking us for an update on others and made us carriers of information in this

---

4.   Stan Swamy, *I Am Not a Silent Spectator*. Indian Social Institute, 2021, p. 106.

wider network of people who may or may not have met before, but who are now intimately connected by a shared destiny.

Even before we got to sit down in the modestly furnished flat in the outskirts of Mumbai, 83-year-old revolutionary poet Varavara Rao had already started speaking about the health of his co-accused in the Bhima Koregaon case, about the conditions of lesser privileged inmates and the kindness he received from others when he was unwell. As a vocal opponent of injustice and the status quo, jail has been a constant feature of his own and his family's life.[5] He recounted the visits in the 1970s and 1980s to his comrades: when he was not himself under arrest, he would go to jail to see his friends, bring them the latest news and talk about politics. He recalled those visits as better and more humane than the *mulaqats*[6] now allowed to the prisoners: they had a longer time together, could sit across a table and eat together and were not separated by a glass wall and forced to speak on an interphone. As Rao reflected on the great sense of isolation and alienation that deeply affects the prisoners while they are inside and cut off from family and community, he also stressed the importance to perceive that there is a network of support and solidarity outside that keeps the memory of their plight and political struggle alive.[7]

This is not dissimilar from what Susan Abraham sees as her life mission. Her destiny is deeply entangled with the fight for justice of political prisoners and in particular with the BK16. She is, in fact, the legal representative of Varavara Rao, Surendra Gadling and Arun Ferreira as well as the wife of Vernon Gonsalves. Susan, whose stern demure hides a heart of gold, was adamant about the fact that she would not be talking to us as a family member.

---

5.   Varavara Rao's wife, P. Hemalatha took over as editor, printer and publisher of the radical literary magazine *Srujana* in October 1973 when Rao was arrested and later acquitted for allegedly being part of the so-called Secunderabad Conspiracy to overthrow the then Andhra Pradesh government. P. Hemalatha was herself jailed three times for her publishing responsibilities.

6.   *Mulaqat* is the term that is commonly used to define the in-person meetings in jail.

7.   Rao was finally granted medical bail on 10 August 2022 after he had been waiting for a decision for over a year as the Supreme Court kept postponing the hearing month after month.

It would be too painful – she said – but mostly because her commitment goes far beyond the personal as it encompasses both the political and the professional spheres.

From an activist perspective, she insisted on the need for tireless campaigning to keep up public awareness. Information around political prisoners gets minimal media attention and is swallowed by the ultrafast news cycle. A headline on a hearing or on worsening medical conditions may pop up for a few hours, outrage thus sparks and dies out and the families are left on their own, sick with worry while they try to disentangle mediatic white noise, bureaucratic loopholes and legal complexities. That is why Susan argued that public mobilisation remains fundamental: to counter the government's obfuscations, to keep media and audiences engaged and alert and to uplift the prisoners' morale so as they feel they are not forgotten.

Speaking as a lawyer, Susan said that there are all the reasons to feel utterly depressed given the pitiful state of the Indian judiciary. There is, however, no feasible alternative other than pursuing legal ways in the fight to free political prisoners. Legal councils need to remain focused and concentrated and be attentive observers of the political situation so as to be able to fine-tune their strategy and keep pace with ongoing transformations. If she works for her husband along with the other prisoners, she manages to stay afloat. Looking at their cases with lucid rationality is her survival mechanism in a situation where finding emotional balance requires relentless effort.

The juggle to 'keep it together' came up in conversations time and again; sometimes with a sad smile, sometimes with the tough attempt to hold back tears. One of the greatest teachings of Paulo Freire is that hope is a political endeavour and an exercise of radical pedagogy that is realised collectively. Nurturing and nourishing hope is both a need and a duty: an act of self-preservation as well as a gesture of care for loved ones. In a mix of defiance and despair, Natasha Narwal wondered whether the moon can be caged forever:

I can also glimpse the moon from our barrack window. It's caged in the grills but the moonlight is coming to us filtering through them. Before coming inside our ward to be locked, I managed to see some stars as well giving the moon some company. I don't know when one will be able to see the night sky without these grills and bars. How long will or can the moon be caged, *hum dekhenge* [We will see].[8]

Natasha told us that the balancing act between hope and despair stayed with her after she was released on bail. Her life outside now has nothing of the life she had always known as her own. She told us that she is one of the lucky ones as she has a tight safety net of love and friendship. Others had it tougher with families and friends reneging on them and cutting ties for fear or disagreement or being forced to live secluded lives and forbidden to interact with former comrades.

For example, activist Amulya Leone's family keeps her isolated at home and does not allow her to interact with anyone other than themselves.[9] The family of Jyoti Jagtap, a BK16 co-accused and a KKM member, believes that their daughter must have done something really bad and 'anti-national' if she's still in jail given that even murderers can get out on bail. For years they refused to talk to her as she brought shame to the family and only recently have considered the possibility of visiting her in jail.

These reactions are harsh but not incomprehensible and occasionally Natasha feels the burden of her actions when she thinks of the consequences they had or may have on her loved ones. There is nothing, however, that would make her reconsider her stance. She said that in this phase of her life it is like being at sea, in the midst of an ocean where stormy waters and gentle waves alternate, requesting to negotiate an always new equilibrium to remain afloat.

In this sea of absence, the sweetness of Sagar's letter offers an anchor of respite. Sagar, Susan Abraham and Vernon Gonsalves' son, writes to his father about a moment of pride that comes from

---

8. This excerpt was published in Natasha Narwal's profile as part of The Polis Project's 'Profiles of Dissent' series. A line from the letter gives the title to this book.

9. We tried to make contact and request an interview but they refused.

the knowledge that people out there are aware of his good work and his commitment to the most disenfranchised both inside and outside prison.

24/5/2022

Dear Dada,

I thought of beginning this letter by some good old-fashioned backscratching. One of my new friends who is doing an LLM at SOAS and is from India was telling me about his experience of working with death row prisoners in Yerwada Jail. He used to work with this organisation called Project 39A that does legal work around the death penalty. Many of the convicts he would come to visit in Yerwada were part of your learning groups! He was describing the change he could see in their approach and interactions with him as a result of your classes. They even had started asking him more questions about the progress of their cases. He was very appreciative of the support you were giving those prisoners. I personally was pissing with pride when I heard this. It was very heart-warming to know that the initiatives you had taken up had led to such tangible changes in the lives of the people around you. It is so inspiring to see how you in the midst of such a terrible situation also continued your work of helping and guiding others. Chalo, now backscratching is done and I will proceed with the letter. ...[10]

Writing letters and waiting for letters is, however, a double-edged sword: since it is a source of hope and love for prisoners and their families, at the hands of a cruel state it becomes a way to exploit their vulnerabilities. Communication with loved ones is a lifeline for prisoners and jail authorities use letters and access to other means of communication as a way to extort obedience, impose submission and enforce their petty authority. Phone or video calls are denied or cut half-sentence; letters are censored, delayed or even withheld. Umar Khalid reflected on this in one of his

---

10. This excerpt was shared with us by Susan Abraham and is reproduced with permission.

letters: 'I wait eagerly for the five-minute weekly phone call or the ten-minute video call twice a week to hear from home. But just as we start talking, the timer ticks off, cutting the call. Never before have I realised the value of every second like I do during such calls to home.'[11]

For Sharjeel Usmani writing was not even an option as he was not allowed to keep a pen or a pencil and paper. For the short while before he got caught, however, Sharjeel managed to hide the writing material inside his pillow. The letter that is published in Chapter 6, 'Voices of Indian Political Prisoners', is one of the few that he managed to entrust to a supportive guard who brought them out of jail and delivered them to his friends. Nodeep Kaur was not allowed to have paper, but she had a pen, so she wrote notes and letters on the front pages of books she borrowed from the prison library. Nargis, the wife of Khalid Saifi, told us that the jail authorities did not allow her to give her husband a drawing that their daughter Maryam had made for him – they just refused and did not give any explanation. Eventually, Maryam asked her mum to draw a message for her father with henna on her forearms so she could take a photo and show it to her dad and no one could take it away from her.

Sahba Husain, who is Gautam Navlakha's life partner, had to go through a score of court petitions to be allowed to communicate with Gautam. As the couple are not married, the authorities used this as a tool to make their life absolutely miserable at every step. It all started the day that Gautam was arrested: since the customary rule, if taken by the letter, technically only allows blood relatives and married spouses to be prisoners' point of contact, their legal counsel had to obtain a special court order to allow for Sahba to be Gautam's. Once this was cleared, the authorities made sure she did not automatically get the right to phone calls, letters and *mulaqats*: even for this she had to request a separate court order.

What may seem only a tedious bureaucratic process has in fact huge emotional consequences: all these legal steps take a lot of time and money. On the one hand, this creates a profound gap between

---

11. This excerpt was published by The Polis Project as part of Umar Khalid's profile in the series 'Profiles of Dissent.'

those who can afford to fight for their right and those who can't; on the other hand, it leaves families for weeks and weeks without news of their loved ones as the authorities intentionally slow down and delay the decision-making process, turning it into a punitive instrument for families and prisoners alike.

Sahba highlighted often how the system is operating in such a way that the pursuit of justice and the recognition of basic rights are turned into privileges that only those who have cultural, social and economic means can afford.[12] While their home is in Delhi, Gautam was jailed in Mumbai: this means that she had to fly and book a hotel every time she went for a *mulaqat*. As Taloja jail authorities allow for a meeting each week, she would generally travel on a Friday, meet Gautam on a Saturday and then take off on a Monday night after going to see him again in the morning, thus making use of the following week's *mulaqat*. She said that at 71, this was a huge cost both financially and physically, but she could not conceive of not going to see him at least once a month. Gautam's lawyers made a request to allow them to have weekly video calls given that the family was not in the same city, but the jail authorities claimed that they did not have the necessary facilities. Even though the legal council contested that this was clearly not true as video call facilities were set up during the COVID-19 lockdown, the jail authorities refused to backtrack and stood by their decision.

This whimsical behaviour of jail authorities makes things unnecessarily complicated, pushing people to believe that this process is in itself a punishment. To further confirm this, Sahba recounted an episode that happened during one of her trips to Mumbai. She had reached the jail early in the morning, took a token to wait for her turn in the meeting schedule and went to stand outside – Taloja has no facility for waiting families and they have to wait in the open irrespective of the heat or the rain with no shelter or

---

12.   When Navlakha was granted a month-long house arrest in November 2022, the Court listed under the conditions that he would himself pay an extortionate amount for the police escort outside his house as well as for the instalment of CCTV cameras outside the door of every room of the house. As of April 2023, Navlakha is still under house arrest in Mumbai.

place to sit. When her turn came, she was told that it would not be possible to see Gautam as he had been taken to hospital for urgent medical checkups. As she walked away and headed to her car, heartbroken as they refused to tell her which hospital they had taken him, she got a glimpse of Gautam through the window of the jail's ambulance. She jumped in the car and, following the ambulance, embarked on a 40-kilometres chase until they reached the J.J. Hospital in South Mumbai.

With a cheeky smile that suddenly lit up her face, Sahba told us that this absurd episode turned unexpectedly positive. Once they reached the hospital she could hug Gautam and sympathetic policemen allowed them to walk hand in hand up the stairs to the clinic and she could be with him all through the process without a glass wall separating them. And here she quoted one of Gautam's favourite lines, where Leonard Cohen says: 'There is a crack in everything. That's how the light gets in.'

To counter the absurdity – if not the sheer cruelty – of jailers and jail authorities, Sahba and Gautam have a recurring joke: they believe that 'people like us' should work as jailers because only they would be able to recognise the prisoners' dignity and treat them and their families with respect.

This reasoning left us both puzzled and admiring of the kind of moral fibre that is needed to be able to think in those terms. It is tough to make light of the relentless persecution meted out to political prisoners and their families and yet people manage to conduct themselves with grace and humanity.

Physical abuses, humiliations and torture of prisoners are the norm. Nodeep Kaur did not want to share details, but made clear that she was herself a subject and a witness of how violent treatment of prisoners is widespread. Things are especially bad for Muslim and Dalit men. Dalit trade union activist Shiv Kumar was tortured using waterboarding and was subjected to constant verbal abuse and casteist slurs. Sharjeel Usmani says that no one speaks about it because they all expect it and take it as a given. Khalid Saifi was beaten with a lathi, urinated upon and waterboarded; Athar Khan was once beaten so badly that even his shoes broke: however horrific, these episodes are by no means an exception.

When not perpetrated through physical violence, abuses find other ways to manifest themselves in jail: Gautam Navlakha has been denied multiple times 'for security reasons' a mosquito net even though he has a history of malaria; Umar Khalid for a long period was not allowed to use his spectacles and G.N. Saibaba his wheelchair. Asif Iqbal Tanha, in somewhat of a bemused tone, recalled the story of newspapers. Inmates are allowed to buy daily newspapers in English or Hindi – but not in regional languages that jailers may not understand – at an increased 'jail price'. The papers, however, would never arrive on the day of issue as they would have to undergo scrutiny and censorship. Asif told us that whenever there was a court hearing or a news article about his case, he would receive the newspaper with gaping holes: a diligent jailer was, in fact, put in charge of neatly (literally) cutting out with scissors any mention of his name.

Cruelty has become such a modus operandi that it is also systematically exercised against political prisoners' families.

Nargis Saifi spoke with immense courage of the challenges of a mother to bring up three children while their father is in jail. Khalid Saifi, who was arrested in connection to the Northeast Delhi pogrom and the anti-CAA protests, has been in jail since 2020 and, as a Muslim man, was subjected to a horrific media smear campaign where he was portrayed as a terrorist. That is when Nargis decided to turn off the TV and stop watching the news as she was worried about the psychological impact this could have on the children. Nargis told us of the huge effort it takes to keep a brave face even when she feels lonely and devastated by the absence of her husband. He had always been the main provider for the family, he would buy groceries, clothes for everyone and even makeup for her. His infectious laughter would fill the house and now, without him, there was an unbearable silence. The arrest was particularly hard on their daughter, who for a long while struggled to sleep as she was in the habit of falling asleep while hugging her father. As a mother, it was difficult for Nargis to make sense of such hardship and, in the early days after he was taken away, she would find herself at the window looking out in the direction from which Khalid would come home, awaiting his return. It took time and determination to pull herself out of that state of suspension as she had to be present and alert for the kids.

There was one moment that almost pushed Nargis to breaking point, it was the last time she took their eldest son to a court hearing. As the boy was about to start boarding school, Nargis wanted him to see his father before he moved to a different city to study. The moment the boy saw his father, he instinctively reached out to touch his arm, but a policeman intervened and violently pushed the boy away 'for security reasons'. Nargis recalled that her son had been brave and strong and never cried once throughout his father's detention – until that day. There and then he started crying and sobbing uncontrollably and kept repeating: 'How can I be a danger to my father?' Nargis was horrified and kept wondering: 'Who is going to answer this?' Such a query is destined to remain unanswered given that the very same authority which is supposedly in charge of protecting citizens seems to derive pleasure from an unmitigated exercise of cruelty.

Noorjahan, Athar Khan's mother, felt the same in court when she saw her son and went to sit behind him so they could be somewhat close. She had a plastic bottle of water in her hands and her son asked for a sip so that, even if indirectly, he could feel his mother's touch. She remembered that she felt her heart melting at her son's request. When Athar reached out for the bottle, however, a policeman slapped his hand and moved him away; Noorjahan felt her soul crush.

The heart-wrenching conversation with Meeran Haider's eldest sister, Farzana, transmitted to us the unspeakable pain that families try to handle in their day-to-day life. She had systematically declined to speak to the media for fear of being tricked or forced to say things she did not intend to or of being outright misrepresented. She agreed to talk to us only because of the intercession of an influential member of the community, who told her that she could trust us. Her pain and sheer effort, however, were palpable when we met her and sat down together in a windowless room. We arrived at her house in the midst of recurring power cuts and, when she started speaking, it was pitch dark even though it was only just early in the morning. Her drone-like voice and muffled sobs emerged from the darkness as the disembodied sound of primordial pain.

We did not stay long as we did not want to inflict further trauma with our presence and questions. Meeran had been in Farzana's custody since he was in 9th grade and now he was in jail. Farzana struggled to make sense of all this. Meeran had always been a good boy and a diligent student if a little too selfless for her own taste. Now Meeran was in jail and her life was upended. Farzana said that he is well liked in the community so even walking around in the neighbourhood at times becomes too difficult as everyone knows she is Meeran's sister and every single time she walks past Jamia Millia Islamia's campus, where Meeran was pursuing his PhD, her eyes well up with tears.

The disruption of life that these targeted arrests brings to families and communities is pervasive and all-encompassing. Reference points are uprooted, certainties wiped out, geographies deterritorialised.

Journalist Rupesh Kumar Singh's son had just started kindergarten when he was arrested and now the boy refuses to go as Rupesh is not there to help him get dressed and drive him to school. Fatima Bathool, the wife of Rauf Sharif, who is in jail in connection to the Hathras case, told us that she was five months pregnant when her husband was arrested. Rauf is still to meet his first child and has not yet seen the house he was building for his family. Varavara Rao was told to live in Mumbai while waiting for his bail hearing, forcing him and his wife to survive with very limited means, so much so that – nodding and smiling towards his wife – he told us: 'I am on bail, but now she is in jail.'

State authorities often operate in the grey area at the edge between legality and illegality: their knowledge of the law is such that they can bend it in seemingly imperceptible ways, wrecking the lives of political prisoners and their families one small abuse at a time. With what comes across as perverse enjoyment, they exercise control over people's lives through the persistent erosion of prisoners' basic rights. Many families told us of the constant worry about the health of their imprisoned loved ones. While there are several international treaties that guarantee prisoners the right to health and adequate medical care, there is hardly any guarantee that people get proper treatment when (more than if) they fall sick.

Structural overcrowding combined with the political decision to only serve (apparently barely edible) vegetarian food and with the complications of the global COVID-19 pandemic make Indian jails particularly unhealthy environments. Most facilities have inadequate medical wards, which are only staffed with Ayurvedic and homoeopathic practitioners. Every family we spoke to told us that irrespective of their ailment, the only allopathic drug prisoners were administered was paracetamol.

On 5 October 2020, activist Atikur Rahman was arrested along with journalist Siddique Kappan, activist Masood Ahmad and taxi driver Mohammad Alam in Mathura, UP. They were on their way to meet the family of a Dalit woman who was raped and murdered by a group of men from a dominant caste in Hathras. The UP Police charged Rahman and others with sedition, promoting enmity between groups, outraging religious feelings, criminal conspiracy under the IPC, raising funds for a terrorist act and conspiring to commit a terrorist act under the UAPA.

In November 2021, Atikur Rahman was admitted to the All India Institute of Medical Sciences (AIIMS) in Delhi for open-heart surgery after his family filed a writ petition in the Allahabad High Court. Since March 2022, he has been hospitalised multiple times. The left side of his body has been paralysed and he suffers from memory loss. Despite the medical advice to shift him to a facility where he can be treated, the Indian state has moved Rahman back to the prison, where the family fears his condition might deteriorate further, putting his life at risk. In September 2022, we received word from his family that along with the partial paralysis of his body, he has now lost vision in his left eye and is reportedly in a wheelchair. His bail hearing was repeatedly postponed and we have been unable to get any updates on his condition.

In April 2021, on behalf of Siddique Kappan's wife, Raihanath, Advocate Wills Mathews sent a habeas corpus request to the then newly appointed Chief Justice of India, Justice N.V. Ramana. Raihanath complained about the inhumane treatment meted out to her husband at Mathura's Medical College Hospital where he was admitted after testing positive for COVID. As his health was dramatically deteriorating, he was chained to the hospital bed 'like an animal', could not eat or use the bathroom and was forced to urinate in a plastic bottle.[13]

Father Frazer Mascarenhas, who was legally appointed next of kin and guardian of Father Stan Swamy, was adamant about the fact that intentional medical neglect contributed to the worsening of Father Stan's already fragile condition and eventually to his death. This was confirmed by the UN Working Group on Arbitrary Detention which in February 2022 declared that his detention was arbitrary and his death utterly preventable.[14] Father Stan was arrested in October 2020 when he was 83 years old and already diagnosed with advanced Parkinson's disease and died in custody on 5 July 2021. During his time in jail, he was made to wait for weeks to obtain the permission to use a sipper – the one he carried was taken away with his other belongings on the day of his arrest – and was thus intentionally deprived of his autonomy and made to depend on the kindness of others:

> ... Arun [Ferreira] assists me to have my breakfast and lunch. Vernon [Gonsalves] helps me with bath. My two inmates help out during supper, in washing my clothes and give massage to my knee joints. They are from very poor families. Please remember my inmates and my colleagues in your prayers. Despite all odds, *humanity is bubbling in Taloja prison.*[15]

Father Frazer is now working to clear Father Stan Swamy's name of all unproven accusations and is advocating for a public investigation into the medical neglect and the deliberate misconduct that led to Father Stan's custodial death.

While remembering Father Stan, Varavara Rao told us that due to the medical negligence of jail authorities he was also pushed to the brink of death. With disarming candour and composure, he

13. Maktoob Staff, '"Siddique Kappan is chained to cot like an animal in hospital", lawyer in an urgent letter to CJI.' *Maktoob Media*, 24 April 2021.

14. Opinions adopted by the Working Group on Arbitrary Detention at its ninety-second session, 15–19 November 2021. Opinion No. 57/2021 concerning Stan Swamy (India), p. 11

15. Stan Swamy, *I Am Not a Silent Spectator*. Indian Social Institute, 2021, p. 100.

recalled the darkest time in jail: he had a urinary ailment for which he needed a catheter that had to be changed every two weeks. The jail authorities ignored his requests and kept the same catheter for two months, which provoked a widespread infection that left him in a prolonged state of delirium and hallucination. He lost memory and control over his body and consequently had to wear a diaper. His family had not been told about his deteriorating health and the severity of his condition until he was already in hospital and they rushed to Mumbai from the southern city of Hyderabad, which is 700 kilometres away. When they eventually managed to see him, they found him on a bed with soiled sheets, semi-conscious and incapable of even recognising his wife. As a monument of integrity and rectitude, Varavara Rao told us all this with no embarrassment or hesitation: his own suffering and physical humiliation had not affected his dignity, instead it had become a damning condemnation of the cruelty of the state.

The moral stature of political prisoners is well acknowledged by their inmates, who are fully aware that they have been targeted for standing up for their ideas. Varavara Rao is convinced that this acknowledgement is particularly infuriating for jail authorities, who rage at them in a (fully unsuccessful) attempt to break their spine and determination. Nargis Saifi one day received an unexpected knock on her door and, when she opened it, found three 'dodgy-looking characters' outside her home. She got a little scared, but the three men turned out to be extremely polite; they refused to enter so as not to put her in an uncomfortable situation and, from the threshold, told her that they had just come out of jail. They had met Khalid there and they wanted her to know that everyone who had contact with him came immediately to understand that he was a genuinely good man. And at this, they left.

Both Sharjeel Usmani and Sudha Bharadwaj spoke about the unexpected clarity that comes from life in jail, the strange grounding it brings and the sense of camaraderie and solidarity they experienced. Sudha is out on bail and cannot leave the city of Mumbai where the NIA filed the case against her. 'I have been displaced multiple times', she told us. 'First from *my* Chhattisgarh, then from my home when I was arrested and now from jail.' After she was released, with the help of friends, she rented a tiny flat where she lives alone except for occasional visits from her daughter who is a university student in a different city. Sudha said that she has always lived in a community: in Chhattisgarh, she was constantly surrounded by fellow activists and trade unionists; in jail, she became Sudha Auntie and – along with Shoma Sen – would help other inmates both with their legal cases and their correspondence.

After her release, for the first time, Sudha was confronted with being by herself, alone in a city she did not know, dealing with a sense of solitude and the need to figure out this new phase in her life. She confessed that the first weeks were incredibly tough, but then Susan Abraham made some space for her in her office so she could resume her legal practice and reconnect with her community through work: things then started taking an easier course.

For people like Sudha, whose sense of self is derived by selfless dedication to others, the return to work and activism is a way to make sense of the world. And she is by no means the only one. Since his release, Sharjeel Usmani has been relentless in his meticulous documentation of individual instances of state abuses against the Muslim community across the country. Nodeep Kaur went back to her struggle for the dignity of daily wage workers soon after she came out. When we asked her whether she was afraid of possible repercussions, she said that now she fights with renewed energy because she owes it to those who supported her work and agitated for her release. She told us that the most difficult thing is the distance that she needs to keep from her partner and her family for their safety: the state has failed in silencing her, but this is the price she needs to pay for it.

In a roller coaster of fear, anger, hope and despair, the community that organically grows around political prisoners, their struggle and liberation is articulating a new collective dimension of the political that counters the increasing cruelty of a markedly fascist state. To homogenising identity politics – both on the left and the right – the diverse network of people that agitates and organises with and for political prisoners responds with a sense of collectivity based on solidarity and mutual care.

The Hindu Rashtra has at its core a politics of dehumanisation that uses political prisoners as a showcase of the extent to which they are prepared to go to hunt down anyone who dares to disagree. The only answer to such horror is the investment in a non-tokenistic inclusivity that acknowledges differences and disagreements, but works towards the common goal of social justice and equal citizenship.

The case of the BK16 proves that the state is terrified by the power and potentials of this kind of transversal solidarity that transcends caste, class and religion and responds to it in the only way it understands: through further violence and further cruelty. If, on the one hand, this deadly escalation puts under severe strain even the toughest of endurances and the brightest of hopes, on the other hand, it bluntly shows that the emperor has no clothes.

While it is true that no state should demand such courage from its citizens, we trust that brutality will destroy its perpetrators faster than it will consume hope and resistance.

5

Small Things

The struggle to pursue justice for those who have been wrongfully incarcerated at the hands of a vindictive state is made of legal battles and campaigns as much as it is of small gestures to keep the memory of political prisoners alive in the public discourse.

To depict a more intimate and humane portrayal, we asked families and political prisoners who are currently out on bail to share with us an object that was meaningful to them or to their loved ones in relation to the experience of jail. Were there small things that they associate with their loved ones during these difficult times, something that gives them hope or strength and renews a sense of proximity and connection when the state tears them apart?

Talking about these little details and ordinary objects became an ice breaker and we saw many a melancholy smile appearing on the faces of family members as if their loved ones were suddenly visible in front of them. Many intimate details came up from these emotional narrations: sweet stories of partners, parents, children, friends and comrades – sometimes funny, sometimes tearful.

These anecdotes contribute to centring the political prisoners, their families and communities beyond public mythology and the icons that they are made to become.

Soon before he was arrested, Athar got his first fully paid employment. With his first salary, he brought fabric for me and his father to make new clothes. The suits are now stitched, but he is in jail. We won't wear our new clothes until the day he will be free.

Noorjahan, Athar Khan's mother

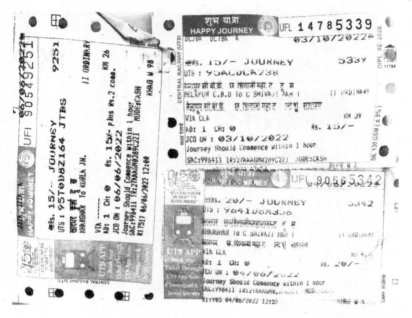

these local train tickets, they lie in my purse most of the time. usually i take the local train while coming back after jail mulaqat. i have been to mumbai with babu when he was outside. even we have gone as a family to visit mumbai. we have travelled in these trains like tourists and now i travel like the wife of a prisoner, going back home without my husband with me.

Jenny Rowena, Hany Babu's wife

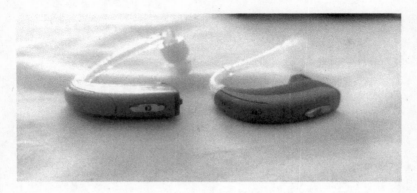

I have kept his last hearing devices with me, he barely used them as he died soon after we replaced them. These devices were very important to Stan as they were a tool for him to stay connected with the people around him.

Father Frazer Mascarenhas, Father Stan's guardian and official next of kin

- Moments before I was arrested, I held my partner's hand and told him that there was something I wanted to tell him. I told him: 'We'll speak about it tonight after the protest.' But then the police took me away and I never got to tell him what I wanted to.
- Can you take a photo of you two holding hands, only a detail of the hands as a memento of this story?
- It may take a very long time.
- How come?
- I don't know where he is, his name has been included in an open FIR on false charges and he is on the run. I have no idea where he is and when I will be able to see him again.

Nodeep Kaur

My daughter Maryam drew a card for her father and wanted me to give it to him when I went to see him in jail, but the guards didn't allow it. She was very upset so when I went back home Maryam asked me to draw it on her arm with henna so no guard would prevent her to show it to her father.

Nargis, Khalid Saifi's wife

Once I brought my son to visit his father in jail. Khalid was very sad that he would see his son after a long time and had no gift for him, so before the *mulaqat* he went to the canteen and bought some sweets and snacks for him from the brand they make in jail.

Nargis Saifi, Khalid Saifi's wife

In our village, you can find different kinds of mushrooms, they are all very good, it is staple food for us here in this part of Jharkhand. Rupesh loves good food and mushrooms are one of his favourite things. Since Rupesh has been arrested, no one in the family eats mushrooms anymore, it just does not feel right. It is not that we spoke about it and decided it, we just don't do it. And this is not only in my home. My mother-in-law does not cook any mushrooms and neither do my own mother and sister. We'll all eat mushrooms again when Rupesh comes back from jail.

Ipsa Shatakshi, Rupesh Kumar Singh's wife

This is a photo of the painting that we have now got framed and keep in our house. It was painted inside prison by one of our co-inmates on 3 January 2021 to mark Savitribai Phule's birth anniversary. She had drawn the image from the postcard that had been sent to us by a Pinjra Tod comrade and we had pasted on the wall of the barracks. It was a conversation starter and way for us to remember that we were part of a larger history of political struggle.

Devangana Kalita

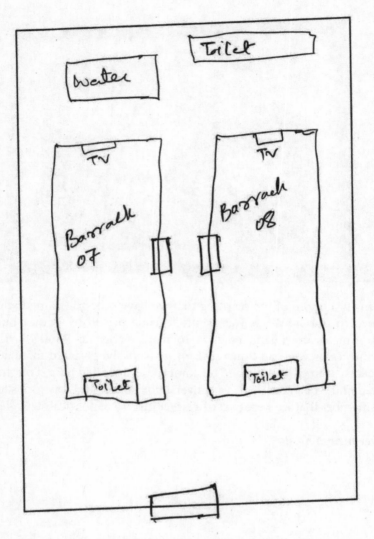

There is a hierarchy in prison as well. In the barracks, the closer you are to the toilet the less privileged you are, the closer you are to the TV the more privileged you are.

Sharjeel Usmani

We were very lucky: Natasha, Gulfisha and I were kept together. From the window of our barrack we could see the moon rise. The three of us are all very fond of the moon, so we would stand together and wait in silence for the moon to show up; the other inmates would laugh as they thought we were a bit crazy. This is the painting of one of the barrack windows Natasha had drawn when we were inside and sent in a letter to friends.

Devangana Kalita

Gautam would buy me flowers every week. When he was arrested, I was torn as I didn't know how to justify to the people he would see everyday that he was no longer around. What should I tell the *phool wala*, the flower seller? Should I lie to him?

I was torn, but I decided to tell him the truth, Gautam sahib is in jail and there is nothing to be ashamed of as he is in jail because of his ideas.

Sahba Husain, Gautam Navlakha's partner

Of course, you can use the photo of the flowers, but you should also include the rocking chair. Everyone who knows Gautam, knows that this is his favourite chair in his favourite place of the house. Here he would sit and read and listen to music and from time to time he would turn around and talk to me as I would sit in my usual spot behind him on the couch.

Sahba Husain, Gautam Navlakha's partner

In jail I only saw a pdf of the chargesheet because there was no place to keep a document that runs for thousands of pages.

Asif Iqbal Tanha

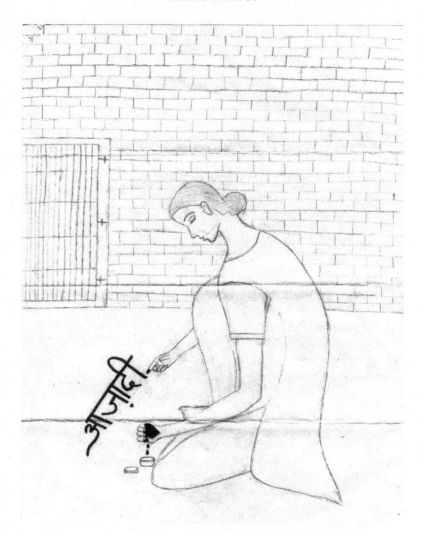

Azadi, freedom is in our blood.

When she writes to us from prison, Gulfisha always sends us poems and artworks. This one says a lot about the kind of person she is.

A friend of Gulfisha Fatima

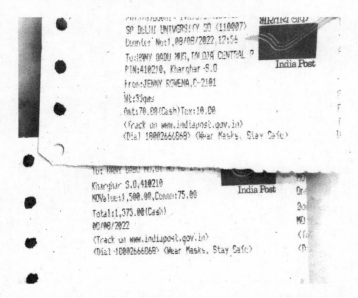

these are the receipts you get at the post office counter. there is a number given in these receipts, which you can use to go online and track your packages. letters in the beginning used to take a long time to reach. esp during covid. then later i would track it and see it has reached but babu would not have got it. some others in the case even gave a petition to the high court regarding not receiving and being able to send letters. now at least the letters we send reach soon. but what babu sends take up to 10 days as though he gives them to post on one day they take their own sweet time to post it. so often me and my daughter we have to read really old letters and yet these letters and these receipts are the most important way in which we communicate. because in these letters at least we can write our heart out. in mulaqats we hardly get 20 minutes and we have to stand across a glass wall and use an intercom to speak. in court visits too we just dont get time to say everything and there are so many people around and the police and so much noise, but in these letters which even if they are reading it, we get the space to say so much. and so these receipts are also so precious. sometimes i cant throw them away even after i know that babu has got my letter.

Jenny Rowena, Hany Babu's wife

6

Voices of Indian Political Prisoners[1]

27 June 1974
Varavara Rao

The moon gets caught in the barbed wire
Over the prison walls
And we, after singing and discoursing,
Lost ourselves in the dreams of revolution

Excerpted with permission from Sweccha *(Freedom), a collection of poems written between May 1974 and March 1977 in Secunderabad, Warangal and Hyderabad jail published in Hyderabad in 1978.*

* * *

1 November 2019
Shoma Sen

Yerwada jail, Pune
March 8

'What is it that these women want?' asked Asthana to himself as he flicked apart two strips of the Venetian blinds of his office window with two pudgy fingers and looked down towards the street below. A rally of a motley group of women carrying placards for International Women's Day and shouting enthusiastic slogans about being Indian women who were sparks of fire and not flowers were marching towards Gandhi chowk. Today itself, coming upstairs in the lift Asthana had been very careful, drawing in his breath to pull his flabby paunch inwards, lest it rub again against the backs of

---

1. The texts in this chapter have been reproduced verbatim.

women standing near him. Ashtana was returning from one of his frequent trips to the Udupi restaurant below which he frequented, to avoid the self-service Dip-chai that made him miss so much, the tea prepared at home.

At home, Shweta was just finishing the morning chores. Ever since they shifted to Bombay from Banaras, Shweta decided to cut down costs and do the housework herself. Seeing the housewives' dress culture here she bought herself four nighties -- two day nighties and two nighties, and put away all her wedding gift saris to wear at special occasions. Today, she ate poha off the kadhai, and got down to scrubbing the dishes. Fifteen minutes later she was on her haunches on the floor, broom in the hand. An obstinate coil of hair kept moving out of reach like a scuttering crab. As she crawled and lunged after it she felt a stab of self-pity. Here she was -- M.Sc first class from BHU, embroiled in nothing but the repetitive motions of housework. She thought of the painting classes she had joined after her B.Sc, before she took music lessons, after her yoga certificate course and her driving classes.

Shweta made herself a cup of coffee and picked up the newspaper. Sweeping aside her husband's pre-office mess: a rejected tie, yesterday's used handkerchief and socks, she sat on one side of the sofa. On the side table, below the lampshade was a photo of the newly-wed Asthanas in a shiny silver frame. She looked at her husband's plump face. His pencil-thin moustache. Two tufts of hair sticking out from behind his ears, curling upwards, the well-oiled locks parted and sleeked to one side and she bit her lip. How hard she had tried to smarten him up, but somehow blue jeans and T-shirts did not help at all. In company, he was usually silent and sounded pompous when he was not. In shopping malls he made the most awful gestures and the shop girls looked patronisingly at his comic moves. If they ate out, he ordered sabzi-roti, which she could have prepared better at home. In bed he had no clue about what gave her pleasure, though he kept trying.

Shweta picked up the newspaper and skimmed through the pages ignoring the headlines, glancing at the weather reports. Mother Teresa was unwell again, her eyes fell upon a small news item about a man being arrested for raping his six year old daughter. The horrifying coincidence was that the incident had happened in her very own building. Waves of discomfort rushed through her veins, as she thought of the child's mother – a slim and silent woman, head covered by the pallu of faded old saris -- whom she sometimes met at the building quadrangle, when the vegetables cart came.

Hot flushes of confused emotions pulsated through her body and mind as Shweta wondered what she should do. On the one hand, she ought to meet the lady, her neighbour and extend her sympathy, offer help of some sort, but then the incident was so repulsive and shameful that she was afraid of intruding upon her privacy. The coffee cup lay unwashed by her side and the newspaper lay unfolded in her lap on her green batik nightie. A gust of wind blew the sheets away towards the bookshelf and Shweta pulled herself together. She had remembered her old college friend Harsha, a women's activist. Harsha, the Bombay girl who came to BHU to study engineering and had been active in student politics. Shweta walked towards the phone and picked up the telephone book.

Harsha arrived just as Shweta finished her lunch. The doorbell rang as she was wiping her washed thali. A fair girl with tousled curly hair and a comical one-sided smile was standing at the door, a large jhola bag pulling her kurta off her shoulder and showing her bra-strap. The old friends hugged and squealed and sighed.

'Want lunch? I just had,' said Shweta.

'I'd love to have something if there is,' replied Harsha. 'I started off in the morning, went to the printing press to pick up pamphlets. Didn't get time to eat only. Today's March 8, no? International Women's Day. We have a meeting in the evening. Why don't you come?'

Shweta told Harsha about what she had read in the papers and her trepidations and anxieties. After Harsha had eaten, greedily licking the dal and rice off the plate with her fingers, savouring the crunchy fried bhindis and aloo choka, they went down the stairs to the first floor. There was a huge lock on the door. Gloom engulfed the landing as thick doors of dark wood and peep-holes stared at each other from three sides, a thoran of silver leaves decorating one door like a sajda.

'Now what?', Harsha exclaimed. 'Maybe she's gone off to her maika after they've arrested him. Must be wanting to avoid reporters and all.'

'Hmm... let's go to your meeting then,' said Shweta.

'You'll come? Fantastic yaar!' Harsha was quite ecstatic.

'Should I change?'

'No men, come like this only.'

In the bus, the two friends tried to catch up on the last few years. Harsha explained to Shweta that she was not exactly married because her partner felt that marriage was a bourgeois institution; a legal certificate necessary only for property matters, and he didn't believe in private property. 'But', she said with a wink, 'he seems to believe in his father's private property because we are staying in his flat right now!'

'And when you have children will they be illegitimate?', asked Shweta, seriously worried.

'We'll cross the bridge when it comes,' said Harsha and continued blabbering about their live-in life. Shweta heard with a smile about how if Harsha cut the vegetables, Dilip cooked, and if he rolled out the chappatis she roasted them and so on.

'What about you?'

'No, nothing great. Typical arranged marriage. He's an MBA.' said Shweta.

Getting off the bus, they walked down the lane to a small primary school in a working class area. The school compound was decorated with posters and banners. A bookstall had been put up where T-shirts and bags with feminist slogans were also being sold. By five o'clock the colourful durries spread out in the compound were full of even more colourfully dressed women and children. There was no stage with chairs on it, no bouquets and no protocol. Everybody sat in a circular shaped crowd. Sushila, a domestic worker who was anchoring the programme narrated the story of the 1908, March 8 when garment workers had marched for their demands: the origin of Women's Day.

It took Shweta a little time to feel at ease in a gathering so differ-ent from the religious and cultural congregations she was used to. Instinctively avoiding the power of women, she squeezed herself into a group of middle class activists and sat down. But soon she found herself getting drawn into the narratives, the experience sharing, so essential to sisterhood groups. Sheela had been a victim of child sexual abuse that had made her extremely introverted and created a feeling of self-loathing. It was her maternal uncle who had raped her one afternoon when she was sleeping alone at home in rural West Bengal. Her employer, in whose house she worked as a maid happened to be a psychotherapist and had helped her heal. Margaret was a staff nurse living in the colony where the meeting was being held, who had left an alcoholic husband and brought up her son single handed, having repeatedly warded off unwelcome advances of other employees in her hospital and at the same time suppressing her own sexual desires. 'My son is a pilot now', she said proudly as if that had made it all worthwhile.

The most horrifying was a story of a dark, stout woman who, in her eagerness to tell her story forgot to introduce herself. She simply got up and threw off the pallu of her sari and said dramatically, 'Dekho!' Her abdomen was criss-cross of scars: puckered flesh and lighter coloured slash lines. 'Dekho usne kaise talwar chalaya mere upar.' Her husband had suspected her of sleeping with his younger brother. Harsha asked Shweta to say a few words. With attention suddenly focused upon her Shweta's throat went dry; she blushed in embarrassment.

'You all are very brave women,' she said simply.

'But today, in my building a terrible thing happened. We must protect our little girls...' and she found herself speaking easily in simple Hindi on child sexual abuse.

Shweta returned home on her own. Throughout the bus journey she kept recounting the experiences of the women in the meeting. She entered the building and ran up to the first floor. The door was still locked. Suddenly Shweta felt a huge sense of relief at the boring normality of her own married life. A surge of tenderness welled up in her heart for her husband. She thought of making something special for dinner that night. Just then the doorbell rang. Asthana was standing there with roses in his hand. 'Happy Women's Day!' he said, 'Shall we go have Chinese for dinner?'

* * *

12 August 2020
Sharjeel Usmani

Assalam Alaikum,

Shukriya [thank you] Mahiya & Usaid Bhai. Received your letter today. Thankyou so much. Glad to know that every thing is fine. I'm also completely well, Alhamdulillah. There's nothing much to do here, therefore, I spend my day mostly reading Maulana Maududi's Tafseer of Quran Shareef which I've arranged from Jail library. Apart from that I have also started paying attention on my health. I plan to gain some weight before I leave jail. Insha Allah. I'm sure Ammi will be pleased to hear this. Say my salam to Ammi & Abbu, Mujtaba Bhai, Afreen, Tahir Bhai, Mamu, Amir bhai, Abul Ala Bhai and All. Have convinced a number of Muslim Youths here to join our movement. Apni Qayadat [our leadership] one day, InshaAllah. Tell her that I miss her, dearly. But be assured that not for one moment have I felt bad for my imprisonment. It is only making me stronger. I'm privileged to have been able to play a small role in our movement. I intend to contribute and learn a lot more. Insha Allah. Please update me what is going outside whenever you write next. Also if possible send me kurta-pyjama, a lungi and a face wash here. Would be very thankful. I get to meet Farhan Zuberi every couple of days for 5-7 mins. Met him just yesterday. He was saying 'Jail aaye ho to faeda uthao kuch' [If you have come to jail, take some advantage from it]. I don't know what he meant by that but I'm sure this would not go in vain. I hope to write in detail about life here once I get outside, Insha' Allah. There's nothing to worry about me here. I am mentally prepared to stay for at least a couple of years if need be. I hope and pray Sharjeel Imam, Asif bhai, Kafeel sb, Meeran and others get bail soon. Insha Allah, our cause and resolution would go stronger with these people as our leader. As for me, I am also preparing myself with all my heart for all the challenges that we may face ahead. There's nothing more certain than the fact that we're all going to change the socio-political equations of this country, and value this country where Muslims lead a life with dignity and equal opportunities. InshaAllah. ATS arrested me, although I should have been arrested by UP police. I hope they're not making me terrorist in media.

Please take care and remember me in Dua [prayer].

Jazak Allah Khair,

Sharjeel Usmani
12-08-20

*   *   *

12 October 2020
Hany Babu

For Sachidanandan[2]

Dear Sachidanandan,

Not as beautiful as it is when outside

This rain seen through the windows of a jail

And It's not like you described

The rain does not rain through glass pipes

The scars on these terraces

It's more than what your 'little angels' can ever wipe

There is not even a single tree here

Even then

They have not been able to take from me the music of this rain

Or silence the deafening sounds of thunder drums

So I lie here listening to its rhythm

On this floor where bandicoots and centipedes crawl

I lie in the warmth of these rough sheets

Not worrying about fundamental rights and basic freedom

---

2.   The reference is to Sachidanandan's famous Malayalam poem *Venal Mazha* written for the then imprisoned Korean poet Kim Chi-ha.

Thinking of my little daughter
Who used to wait for me to come home, every night
And my wife
Who is now bearing the burden of the house
Thinking that i am not alone in this iron barred-prison
I go to sleep in this prison now
Dreaming of a country
Where our fundamental rights and freedoms
Are not snatched from us
And where we can sit watching the glass pipes of the rain

--end--

Translated from Malayalam with permission.

*　*　*

December 2020–January 2021
Asif Iqbal Tanha

To,
The Suprintendent,
Central Jail No. 4,
Tihar, New Delhi–64,
Sub: Application requesting transfer to Seperate cell in W/15

Respected Sir,

My name is Asif Iqbal S/O Mujeebullah. I'm currently lodged in ward 9/2 of your jail. The atmosphere in ward is not suitable for me. Anyone who got to know my case details starts acting strange with me. I'm a student and I'm unable to focus on my studies. Almost everyone around is a hardcore criminal or a history sheeter. In my case alot of media trail is happening and my name appears in every newspaper every other day.

My co-accused Athar Khan S/O Afzal Khan is also experiencing same thing. (Athar's signature)

I request you to take appropriate action in our matter. We'll be obliged to you.

Thanking You,
Yours' Obidiently,
Asif Iqbal
S/O Mujeebullah
Ward – 9/2

* * *

14 March 2021
Natasha Narwal
Date – 14/03/21

Dear Sistaahs...

It has been a while since I have written to you. coz I have been too busy and a bit lazy. :p Recently, I got Jo's and Medhavi's letters and it brought so much joy and warmth along, both in their character-istic writing style with so much love. Uff! Cuties!

Khair (anyway), now that I am finally writing, another season has passed and ~~it is~~ the much awaited spring is here. Though, annoyingly the small bouganvilla bush which had finally started blooming fully has been cut. And Champa is not growing much either. There was very short appearance of white guldoodi (chry-santhemum), like a cameo and some more flowers here and there. Mind often war wanders to the walls of JNU overflowing with bouganvillas, the burst of colours everywhere, our photo-ops and flower collection. :) The city must also bursting with the bright red of semal [*Bombax malabaricum*]. [I am sure D must have already mentioned all of this in the letter she is writing simultaneously. Uff yaar [friend], she is so annoying. I requested her that as she has already written to you guys last month, let me write this time. So, like our letters will be mostly similar I guess, :/]

It's the season when you can't figure out if you want the fan on or off and its a source of lot of tiffs in our barrack as D always wants the fan on while others feel cold, and diff people want it on or off at various points in the day when the others don't want. :P

It's also the season of 'returnings' in here as all the inmates who had gone out on interim bail due to Covid are coming back. It's such a strange sight to witness, people greeting each other with much warmth and excitement but also disappointment of seeing them in jail again. ~~One new~~ It almost feels like people are returning to hostels after the breaks :p.

Jail is a strange place to forge friendships. The joy of ~~some~~ someone's rihai (release) also brings the pain of parting with no promise of meeting again but you can't wish for them to stay either. Once me and D were discussing how you can't sing the usual parting songs like 'Aaj Jaane Ki Zidd' (today, insist on leaving) or 'Abhi na jao chod kar' (do not leave me now) etc and we really couldn't figure out what to sing as we bid farewells to some dear ones, especially some kiddes as they [were] too excited and hesitant steps towards the outside world. A world which is mostly an enigma for them as most of them grew up here. We could only hold their tiny hands ~~thr~~ through the bars of our barrack gate for a few seconds. Little L, who was quite obsessed with D, used to be mortally scared of 'uncles' and we used to tease him that What will he do outside as there are so many uncles ~~in~~ outside. Hope he has adjusted to their presence and eating chocolates and ice-creams as he had told us he would. Now, the two little ones remain and I don't know what I'll do without them when they leave but I can't wish for them to stay here. Uff! So complicated yaar (friend).

let me tell you guys about the most exciting thing, which is celebrating Women's Day in jail with 'Tod Tod ke bandhano Ko' (break-break the fastenings) reverbrating in the air. Uff! ~~I~~ it was so amazing and I missed all of you ~~randomly keeps singing ' Nidar azaad ho jayengi, wo toh naya zamana layengi ' from across the barrack door. This is her favourite line apparently.~~ like crazy. We (the 3 of us, basically we are considered one unit) were given the task of preparing a short play for the 8th March program. Having never done that, we were quite nervous. The script and all the dialogues had to be pre approved by the authorities, so our options were quite limited. :p After taming our wild ideas, we came up with a rather simple script. Taking cue from an Urdu play G had read long back came the idea of an old king whose power lies in a snake whom we called 'Sikka' who thrives on the blood derived from women's oppression and exploitation. But these days he is unable to get his usual portion of blood and is getting weakened. The angry king summons his mantri (minister) and orders him to get adequate portion of blood for Sikka. As the mantri minister goes in search of blood, he is encountered with 3 situations where women are being put in different kinds of bandhans (restrictions). In the first, one, a girl is being helplessly told by her mother that she can't afford to get her educated as the social and economic constraints have bound her. The mantri minister is happily deriving blood from this situation when suddenly Savitri Bai and Fatima Sheikh enter the scene and question why the girl is being stopped. As the The mother excitedly asks who they are and the characters introduce each other and their struggles for women's education and against caste oppression. T

The mantri's minister's attempts in the second situation where two women are being told by their father that they can't take up employment are foiled by Rani Laxmi Bai and Jhalkari Bai as they proudly assert that if women can fight battles why can't they work outside their homes. And in the third situation, where a young woman is being told that she can't fall in love and marry by her choice, Sarojni Naidu and Bibi Fatima intervene and tell the women that our Constitution gives her autonomy. In anger and bewilderment the king demands these women to be presented before him and all the characters reappear on the stage singing 'Tod Tod ke bandhano ko'. They end the play with the slogan of 'Nari Shakti Zindabad' (long live, female power). Though in hindsight I feel it should have been 'Nari Mukti zindabad' (long live, female power). :p

The play was a hit and was appreciated by everyone, including the ██████████ who was a special guest that day. But the most exciting and heart–warming process was the week-long preparation, where so many women took their first hesitant steps but excited steps towards entering different characters, understanding and owning them and the play. For most of them, this was their first time being on stage, speaking in front of people and being introduced to these ~~diff~~various women from history and their struggles.

For that one week, it really felt that the walls, the locks around had disappeared and we all were somewhere else, floating in history and a new future at the same time. Different barracks resonated with sounds of 'Tod Tod ke bandhano Ko' and dialogue practices ~~in~~ at night. The one who played Savitri Bai lives in the barrack opposite ours and one night while practicing shouted from across the corridor 'tum teeno ne mujhe jail ki hawa laga di hai' (you three have made jail affect me). :p ███████████████ whose education was stopped when she was quite young as it was deemed useless for girls. It is here in prison that she has begun to learn to read and write again. She has become quite an avid reader. When I was working in the library, she would come and demand something new to read every second day. :) I had given her some old Nirantar magazines that I had found, to read and she loved them. She had especially loved reading extracts from Sultana's dream and life story of Savitri Bai.

And here she was, playing Savitri Bai on Stage. Initially, she was extremely hesitant and kept saying 'Hum nahi kar payenge behni, hum itne logon ke saamne kabhi nahi bole hain' (I will not be able to do this, sister, I have never spoken in front of so many people). But her fluttering voice transformed gradually into confident assertion of Savitri Bai and she delivered a steller performance. She keeps humming 'Tod Tod ke ~~ke~~ bandhono Ko' every now and then from her barrack. Her favourite line is 'Nidar azaad ho jayengi, wo toh naya zamana layengi.' (they will become fearless and liberated, they will usher in a new era)

Another friend, who played the role of the mother who has to tell her daughter that she can't study, broke down after one of the rehearsals as everytime she would perform the scene, her kid's faces would flash in front of her. As she was the primary ~~brea~~ earner and care-taker in the family, her absence has meant that there is no body to look after them and ensure their education. They have stopped going to school and her husband is an alcoholic who is least bothered.

She wants to send them to some government ai school cum hostel but the husband refuses to let her even do that because of his own insecurities. She has been feeling extremely helpless and frusturated and breaks down often staring at a blank and bleak future. But she gathered herself so gracefully and did an amazing performance on the final day.

The woman who played Sarojini Naidu has been here and this was her first time performing on stage. Though she really wanted to be in the play, it was quite a task getting her for the rehearsals and making her speak loudly, and led to some sore moments. But in the final performance she spoke with full confidence and loudly ~~as she~~ about the Indian Constitution's guarantees of a non-discriminatory and autonomous life for all its citizens. A few days back she told me how that peformance has given her voice and she is not going to let anyone take her for granted and fight for herself. [Khamoshi aur gham ko milkar peeche chodengi ...] (together they will leave behind silence and sorrow)

16/03/21

One of my favourite moments in the whole process was when during one of the practice sessions, where everyone was absorbed in singing, two women suddenly realised that they have to go for their work to peel matar (peas) for the food preparation in the langar (kitchen). They didn't want to go but didn't know what to do. After a few moments of confusion, other women asked them to stay and offered to help in the work later so that the work can be compiled on time. :)

[Haan Meri Behenein Ab milkar khushi manayengi ...] (yes, my sisters will now celebrate happiness together)

It was such a beautiful process of building solidarities and sisterhood. One women, who played the role of the Raja (king), is a very open woman whom everyone calls Mummy Don. She wants to open a Natak [drama] Company when we all go outside. :P But it was also a process fraught with a lot of inter-personal tensions, undercurrents of everyone's own bagagges which can't all be shared. Holding everything together was quite a task and at times one didn't know what to do or how to do it. It was also a reminder of how building any kind of collective is never an easy or a smooth

process. It always involves the complex web of emotions and nego-
tiating the said and unsaid, structure and agency. :P It was also a
realisation that how inadverently one resorts to the usual sources
of power, external and one's own. I don't think I have ever shouted
at people as I did during this whole process when people wouldn't
show up for rehearsals for hours. However frustrating that process
was, the fact remains that I could shout because well I could, as
people vest a certain authority consciously and unconsciously in
people of our social location. In one very shameful moment, in a
moment of extreme frustration, I asked one of the 'madams', to ask
people if they really want ~~do~~ the play and if yes, then they should
come on time.

It has really been a lesson in how much one needs to work on the
self and continuously, on these internalised power structure and
hierarchies, to create more meaningful amd equal solidarities. How
our task is to never cease working on the self and the collective,
no matter if we are inside or outside these walls. How even inside
the prison walls, sounds of ~~women's~~ our songs, our laughter, our
slogans can echo. [Naachengi aur gayengi who falkaren dikhlay-
engi] (dancing and singing, they will show stars).

Az Nazim Hikmet says... 'Being captured is beside the point. the
point is not to surrender.' And we haven't and neither will surrender. And I hope and believe that neither will you.:)

Many of you are back in the city as we were told. ~~Ho~~ Write to us
about that. How does it feel to inhabit those ~~sf~~ same spaces in such
a different context. Has it provided some comfort and warmth of
companionship or does it only feel strange. Oh and also thanks
a ton for such lovely birthday wishes. I did have a very pleasant
day which mostly went in play preparation. Nibs and Andre paid
a surprise visit and at the end of the day I cut two jail style cakes
which a friend had made with lot of love and effort. As I cut the
cake, someone started shouting 'Nari Shakti Zindabad'. :P So, there
was sloganeering as well. The two little kiddies were going around
saying Happy to you Natata and we danced together. I got countless duas (prayers) for rihai (release) by various inmates and all the
staff members as well. :) How did the zoom party go for you guys.
Please to give gossip and details. Hehe!

And you know this D and G have teamed up against me and keep bullying me all the time. First they irritate me and then if I shout at them, they say you are shouting at us and they stick notes on the wall that I shouted. D plans to call it Wall of my crimes. :/ But I guess I should forgive them as they are not productively employed like me na.

Khair, this letter is becoming longer than I thought so I'll give more details about this experience in my next letter. For now, I'll end with some beautiful lines which are written as a dedication in the Prison Memoirs of Nawal el Sa'adawi, an Egyptian activist, which Aakash has recently sent me. ~~Ang~~ And you peeps also, please send me more prison memoirs by women yaar. :p

> 'To all who have hated oppression to the point of death.
>
> Who have loved freedom to the point of imprisonment.
>
> And have rejected falsehood to the point of revolution.'

So amazing and powerful na. Chalo (anyway) ok byeeeeee.

Lots and Lots of love and Hugs.

Natata

P.S. – Sorry drawing banane ka time nahi mila (sorry, did not get the time to create the drawing) but it's in the making. :)

*   *   *

7 April 2021
Father Stan Swamy

Light, Hope, Love – The New Order
Light overpowering darkness
Hope replacing despair
Love winning over hate
Is the message of Jesus risen

> Darkness, despair descended on me
> At lower court declaring me complicit
> Of waging war against the State
> As such not deserving bail

And what was the evidence?
Some documents planted in my computer
Which were supposedly addressed to me
Something I myself was not in the know
>My co-accused colleagues
>Assured me this accusation is nothing new
>They too have been accused similarly
>I was thus consoled to be in their good company
But fight we will till the end
Not so much just to save our skin
But to speak truth to power
Counting all the while you all are with us in mind and heart.
Stan Swamy

(This poem was posted by Fr. Stan on 7 April to Fr. Joseph Xavier and received on 27 May, just the day before he was permitted by the Court to be admitted in Holy Family Hospital, Bandra).

Excerpt from Stan Swamy, I Am Not a Silent Spectator. *Indian Social Institute, 2021, p. 110.*

* * *

8 April 2021
Surendra Gadling

Dear Kanchan,

You cannot read this letter written to you and no one can read and show you this letter. This letter cannot reach you because you are no more.

You are not amongst us, gone from this world. Your continuous struggle with seven years of imprisonment and your terminal illness/asthma has come to an end today.

This fascist system has taken your life! Your death is an institutional murder, as I understand. That is why this letter cannot reach you, of this I am aware.

But this letter will surely reach all the care filled with your memories. This letter will reach all those eyes whose embers burned in your martyrdom.

I trust that this letter will reach every fist raised against the fascist regime.

Your optimism to live and continue to fight against this anti-people power while living and to win this basic struggle of revolution sooner or later was really elevated. That lofty, lofty optimism of yours will continue to sustain us today to live and fight.

It is said that one should not talk or write about the case while the case is in progress. But today I have to break these rules.

Because while waiting for this case to end, you went away without saying anything.

But I will have to say something because I cannot wait for the case to end.

At least, not now. Because I might die tomorrow while I wait for the case to end. Then who will speak on this subject on my behalf?

Your tenacity was truly invincible. Neither prison, nor repression, nor this disease, none could break you from the movement to end caste-class-female slavery.

Everyone wants to live life, so did you. But your will to live was overshadowed by social sensibilities.

Your life's will blossomed on world-changing revolutionary ideology.

Then your will to continue fighting will become a fragrance. The flowers of revolution that have blossomed through your life's journey will never wither.

These flowers will continue to swirl around us with their optimism and inspiring fragrance. Kanchan, as a human rights activist lawyer I want to apologize to you. Because I failed in trying to rescue you from prison. Activists like you give your all to the people's movement.

Jails, treason cases are going on floor to floor without any care. You keep walking without stopping, trampling over many bumps and thorns, sometimes with the system, sometimes with your family, sometimes with yourself and sometimes with the situation.

At such times, the system systematically tries to block your journey, suppress you, intimidate you and deter you from this path by entanglement in court-offices and prisons. So, in this kind of crisis, in this battlefield of 'state power against you', as a lawyer on your side as your defense, as a responsible person. You have to fulfill your responsibility in the movement. For the past twenty-five years I have been fulfilling this responsibility as a human rights lawyer/activist.

Throughout my twenty-five years of legal career, I have worked with integrity and determination to bring justice to my clients.

I have been fighting the cases of political prisoners which have been the main focus of my life. It was my social sensibility, which has supported me to fight as their lawyer to give them justice in political cases.

But in this Elgar Parishad case, I myself have been in jail for the last three years, so I fell short in trying to free you, I am very sorry for that. Kanchan, I will definitely review this case.

I will keep asking my sensitivity that where and why did I fall short in trying to rescue you from prison? Your departure will remain a guilty wound on my mind.

Kanchan, you gave your life very thoughtfully in the mass movement and lived the fakir's life till the end.

You were determined and remained determined till your last breath to create a caste-less society based on equality by eradicating the injustice and oppression imposed on the people by the caste-agnostic regime.

So, I can say with certainty that in the mass movement for just rights, a fist of yours raised in hatred in the march will be raised in the same manner as you breathe your last!

We read the histories of Savitribai Phule, Shahid Bhagat Singh, Dr. Babasaheb Ambedkar and store it in our consciousness, salute their revolutionary life, and consider them as role models and try to follow their footsteps.

From this point of view, you seem to have taken a lot of steps forward in this journey and I am proud that we are now following in your footsteps.

I see the noble history of revolutionaries living in the present in your form.

Not an exaggeration of my feelings because as a human rights lawyer in the last twenty-five years I have seen the movement to end caste-class-female slavery and the fearless and determined activists of this movement. I have experienced your journey in this movement.

I have heard and seen your struggle as a political prisoner in Chandrapur and Yerwada jails. When your family raised the question of moving home, you sacrificed your home and devoted your life to the movement, so I salute (Jai Bhim) your revolutionary life and fierce life struggle.

Jai Bhim, a revolutionary from the heart, not as a mourner!

Kanchan, if you were out of jail, you could have saved yourself by getting better treatment. Such serious illness requires loving and sensitive people from home, who will help wholeheartedly.

You could have received such help to recover from illness outside of prison. But maybe we failed to convince the court! And left you at the mercy of the prison administration, who do not know the difference between a prisoner and an animal.

Kanchan, it is definitely not easy for you to go like this. I consider your death to be a planned institutional murder, as an under-trial detention.

You have spent almost seven years in Yerwada jail under very difficult conditions in the hope of justice. During these seven years, your bail application on medical grounds was kept on hold by the sessions court and the high court in a game of delayed dates ('date to date' refers to the consecutive dates given by the courts for hearing case).

A major reason for denying you bail lies in the capitalist-Brahminical, caste-based system and the vested interests of this system of governance and administration.

Today, BJP and Sangh-related criminals and rioters are given a clean chit, freed from jail and freed from trial. A senior police officer in Kashmir has been granted bail in three to four months in a case of terrorism-related charges. An editor associated with the BJP gets bail in a criminal case within days. The Bhima Koregaon riot accused Bhide is not even arrested, and Ekbote gets bail within a month.

But Kanchan Nanavara is not getting bail for seven years despite suffering from terminal illness. Also, Vara Vara Rao, part of the Elgar Parishad case, is also not getting bail.

The accused in this case have been in jail for almost three years. Students protesting constitutionally against anti-people laws like CAA and NRC are jailed.

Bail is rule, jail is exception.

It is an undisputed basic principle of criminal jurisprudence that a person is innocent until proven guilty. And there is no doubt that Bail is rule, Jail is exception is the principle evolved by the court.

But this basic principle of justice could not come to your aid. Because these principles are being used in a selective manner according to convenience.

These principles are guaranteed to bring justice to BJP-Sangh sidekicks and stakeholders. The biased nature of the Indian system to grant relief from courts is visible internationally. You have also become a victim of this.

So, your death is definitely not simple. Your death is a festive slap in the face of this biased system.

A slap that will continue to reverberate in the ears of the brokers and biased system that is becoming conveniently deaf to all the oppressed.

Kanchan, in the end I'll just say you're gone! But as a martyr, you will live on as an invincible revolutionary in every race that sets out to change the world.

To you, a revolutionary Jay Bhim!
Your friend, an activist/political prisoner
Advocate Surendra Gadling MB 98,
U.T. No. MB 98
Circle No. 2/5 Taloja Central Jail

This letter, addressed to the late Dalit-tribal activist Kanchan Nanavare accused of having links with the Naxalite movement, was originally published in Marathi in Indie Journal. *Following serious medical negligence, Nanavare died in police custody on 24 January 2021. The letter is translated and published from Marathi with permission.*

* . * *

21 May 2021
Athar Khan

As-salamu-alaikum,

   Once again, Eid Mubarak... How is everyone? Alhamdulillah, Ramadan is going to finish and I have also observed all fasts. Initially, I thought it would be very difficult to fast in jail but if fast is easiest somewhere in the whole world, then it is probably in jail. Every day, freshly made, hot and great food comes in for Sehri [meal before dawn] on time around 3 AM. And for Iftar fritters, sometimes fried lentil dumplings, sometimes samosa or moong dal halwa, and we ourselves do the arrangement for fruits.
Well, this is the story of jail.... You tell me, what are the conditions outside? Will Eid prayers be held this year or would it remain like last year? And tell Imam Sahab to remember me in prayers with name. And if you meet any of my mosque companions, tell them that I missed our mosque's *dastarkhan* [cloth used for serving food on the floor] a lot...

Now, a matter of importance.... The Eid of three little ones should be best, as according to the situation outside. Don't let my presence or absence spoil their happiness. Maybe not this time, but Inshallah will celebrate the next Eid together. Though, I miss everyone daily, but I missed more in Ramadan. How much ruckus we used to create at dawn and Iftar.

Well, it doesn't matter. There is some prudence in each act of Allah.

Mom-Dad, take care of your health.

Bilal, keep calm and fix the long beard you have kept.

Jawwad, leave the clumsiness, become wise and focus on studies.

Anas, stop looking at phone so much and focus on studies.

Now, they are not putting money through the CPRO [Central Public Relation Office]. Money is only coming by money order. Do not waste your time and do not risk contracting COVID-19 by coming here.

Tell salaam to everyone from me and tell my friends I am verbally abusing them that they could not write anything in these 10 months and even now, just keep thinking.

Alright, take care of yourself. Love you all.

Allah Hafiz

From,

Athar

Translated from Hindi with permission.

* * *

2 November 2021
Sagar Gorkhe

Date

To the Honorable

Justice Special NIA

Court

Court Room No.

Mumbai Session

Court Mumbai

Applicant: Sagar Tatyaram Gorkhe

Subject: Immediate Action against Mr. U T Pawar Superintendent of Taloja Jail for harassing the applicant with a vengeance.

Respected Sir,

On 26/09/2021, Superintendent Mr. U T Pawar came on a round to hear the grievances of the jail inmates as per his regular duty. He came for the round in the closed yard which was muddy and clogged with water due to heavy rains. He was standing there taking the grievance applications from 9/10 jail inmates. He was listening to them and giving decisions.

Three days prior to this i.e. on 23/09/2021, during the search operation, my important documents, circular and jail manual belonging to me were stolen by some officer and were burnt. I was standing along with other inmates to make a complaint regarding this. All the inmates were told to remove their footwear and stand in the muddy water. I refused to remove my footwear and the following argument happened with the superintendent –

Sup. – Hey remove your chappals. Don't you understand you have to remove your chappal?

Me – Sorry sir but is it necessary to remove the chappals?

Sup. – What do you mean by necessary? Don't you know that you do not wear chappals during the rounds?

Me – Why should I remove my chappals at a public place? I do not even remove the same in the court.

Sup. – But here you have to remove in front of the superintendent.

Me – But this is against the rules. I am a Dalit and with these instructions I feel that I am standing in front of the village Patil's (chief/wealthy person) bungalow. I feel humiliated. I will not remove the chappals.

Sup. – Hey, don't talk about Dalit and all. Here everyone is equal.

Me – Where is the equality sir, you are wearing your shoes and asking me to remove my chappal in this water and mud. This is like following caste system.

Sup. – Don't give a lecture. Are you going to remove your chappal or not?

Me – Sorry sir, I feel humiliated. I will not remove.

Sup. – OK then I will not hear your grievance/request.

After saying this to me Mr. U T Pawar left with his staff. Since that day the Superintendent has been harassing me.

All my ayurvedic medicines for skin disease, Arthritis and Psychotherapy have been detained / stopped. I was taking all these medicines since last one year. All my treatment has been stopped.

He has stopped giving me hot water for a bath which I used to get for the treatment of my arthritis and skin disease.

I was tested positive for covid. Since then, I have been not keeping well. The superintendent has stopped my medical diet started by the medical officer.

I am also not allowed to do any correspondence and meet the lawyer who listens the problems faced by the jail inmates.

All the books, clothes, stationary, post stamps which have been bought by my own expenses have been detained.

I am being warned and not allowed to talk to the co accused.

Request – Only because of his ego, Mr. U T Pawar has cornered me and has been harassing me. I request the honourable court to look in to this matter to stop my harassment and take necessary action.

Date: 02-11-2021

Signed – Sagar Tatyaram Gorkhe

Translated from Marathi with permission.

* * *

1 January 2022
Sudhir Dhawale

This cruel era which brings with it the loss of man
This 'Big Brother' era of blatant and nude capitalism
The stray dogs of sadness and sorrow roam nearby in this fearful period

With defiance in their eyes, the students roared '*Hum dekhenge* – We will see'

The silent scream for survival by Muslim women, Shaheen Bagh! Shaheen Bagh!

The flames of justice have been ignited in Hathras and Bhima Koregaon

'We will not die! We will fight!'

A people's war has been won by peasants in the past

The source of happiness is found in the pain of sorrow

Rebellion gives birth to equality in men

During times of intense fear, the appreciation for freedom and colourful flowers arises

Even in the land of uncountable bloodbaths

The Sun always shines.

By

Sudhir Dhavale

1st January 2022

Taloja Central Jail

Translated from Marathi with permission.

* * *

21 May 2022

Ramesh Gaichor

My dear Mosquito Net

My dear Mosquito Net
You were very dear to me
So much so that I can't explain
Trapped in this scary uncomfortable prison,
Sleeping in your embrace
Made me feel better.

I saw a lot of dreams because of you.
Dreams
To live in this hellish environment
Dreams that gave support,
Dreams, that gave me humanity,
Dreams that gave the inspiring optimism of Phule Shahu Ambedkar,
Dreams, that said Bhagatsingh, Sukhdev, Rajguru,
And painted a fervent picture of tomorrow!
My dear Mosquito Net!
Though you're inanimate,
I still felt you're more alive than the living,
In this prison's inhuman crowd,
You met me in the form of humanity,
But
Dear Mosquito Net,
Now you're not with me
You've been forcibly taken away from me,
By some enforcers,
On the orders of their cold-hearted master
Ignoring all my requests
Flouting the rules of the jail manual,
Insulting the Supreme Court's judicial perspective.
Even though you were necessary for me
You've been painted as a threat for me
Conspiring with the mosquitoes
You've been snatched from me
Now these malaria-, dengue-carrying mosquitoes
Will drink my blood,
Take my life.
My death has become cheap,
For an under-trial prisoner's death,

Who will be responsible?
Dear Mosquito Net
When you were by my side
I slept peacefully
But now,
I'll stay awake, disturbed and restless
And
The person who is restless,
Disturbed,
And sleepless
Is the one who is always fighting for his rights
The officer who's snatched you away from me
would not be aware of this
Ramesh Gaichor
   Taloja Central Prison
   High Security Ward
   Date: 21.05.2022
   At night, 9:30 pm

Translated from Marathi with permission.

*   *   *

24 May 2022
Gulfisha Fatima

On 24-May-2022. At night there was raining and I was awake so these lines I penned down immediately.
Yesterday in the black night,
On the doors of prison,
There was a knock,
Of innocent winds,
Of echoes of loved ones,

The lightning too,
Screaming to appeal for mercy,
Demanded our release,
The mourning of delicate branches,
Was included,
In public,
After the unsuccessful attempt,
Became uncontrollable,
Began flowing,
The tears of fragile rain,
Clashing with drum of the earth,
The thump of raindrop,
Raised the,
Uproar of complaints,
However,
The deaf serpents,
Kept dancing with,
Venomous fangs unfurled,
The barbed web spread,
And,
The oppressed kept their hands raised,
Yesterday in the black night.

Translated from Hindi with permission.

* * *

29 May 2022
GN Saibaba

29.05.2022
My Dearest Vasantha,

How are you? This enquiry has turned cruel in these days of darkness and tyranny. This natural question now cannot be written or asked naturally without a troubling mind.

I know you must be angry with me for I went on Hunger Strike, though you always say I mustn't. What can I do? My circumstances have had no options and I was compelled. On the evening of the fourth day, I agreed to withdraw my hunger strike after the second CCTV camera installed was tilted its direction away from prison cell.

The four-day Hunger Strike (21 May to 24 May) was much more difficult due to the heat waves and my failing health condition after two serious attacks of the coronavirus in the past one year. Yet, I would have continued my hunger strike, had the first and second cameras were not removed or changed direction.

On the third day started blood motions uncontrollably. The Skin on my hands and other parts of the body became loose and wrinkled. My head was spinning and I was losing consciousness on and off.

After I withdrew the strike, I was given treatment in the hospital of the prison. I.V. fluids were injected with medicines, mainly anti-biotics for two days. Then, slowly blood motions have stopped and recovered from the fatal stage a little bit.

Now after that I have been taking ORS and Glucose in every few hours. Our Advocate also brought Glucose packets and electral packets (ORS) apart from the CMO of the hospital sent ORS packets and Glucose.

* * *

11 August 2022
Vernon Gonsalves

Sometime back a newspaper that comes to the jail carried an aerial photograph of the Taloja Central Prison (you'd probably get in on Google). Very few of the prisoners here could not at first sight, recognize their 'home'. It seemed like one of those pretty pictures in advertisements for holiday homes and picnic resorts – separate neatly distempered dwellings at the foot of a picturesque hill, verdant surroundings, green grass, gentle looking trees.

The close-quarter reality is of course quite different. Prisoners are penned into grey mildewed concrete enclosures, rarely allowed the sight, never allowed the touch and feel of the greenery outside. They are perpetually squashed within squalid, overcrowded, smelly, leaky, damp, unventilated barracks, each set carrying hundreds of humans sharing space with thousands of flies and mosquitos, and millions of ants.

That aerial photo is a tempting metaphor for the average prisoner who, with valiant bravado, puts up an amiable sunny disposition that barely can conceal a soul sunk in a cesspool of despair.

The case of political prisoners can however be somewhat different. Their commitment to a cause or the call of their conscience helps to trump the lows of imprisonment and its attendant disabilities. The unjustness of incarceration finds some match – at least in the political prisoner's mind – in the justness of the greater battle she is waging or wanting to wage.

Then, she is also often an activist with the natural activist tendency to get immersed in minimising the miseries of those around. In a place like prison with distress aplenty that is a 24/7 mission. In a place where professional prison counselling help is unknown, you lend a sympathetic ear and a comforting shoulder, and even try some amateur counselling; where the doctor is either absent or absorbed in only attending to those who can bribe, you advise on what medication to take and, more importantly, what to avoid; where legal aid is a myth; you become the jailhouse lawyer explaining chargesheets and deciphering judgments, drafting applications to authorities and petitions to courts; and where basic human rights are eclipsed and scorned, you persuade and prod the prisoners to protest and prise out some semblance of humaneness from a soulless system. All this can be hard work. It creates and sustains a camaraderie that is particularly precious in prison life. Happily, it doesn't leave you the time or the inclination to cry.

Not all political prisoners are however that lucky. Recently a court in the state of Chhattisgarh acquitted 121 tribal villagers who had spent several years in prison in a Maoist case. Journalists who met them on their release at the prison gates and later in their villages found most in states too numb for any celebration of freedom. The days in prison had taken too heavy a toll from them and their families. Most were young and would take some time to piece together their lives.

Something similar happens to many of the thousands of Muslim political prisoners in jails throughout the country. A large number have been picked up after just a chance meeting with someone under watch or for a curious foray into a forbidden website. In their teens or barely out of them, they have been implicated in major terror cases and consigned to solitary cells, while prosecutors purposely prolong trials for ten to fifteen years and then appeals for many years more. Freedom in the forties has a different taste after a youth behind bars.

A recent reply to a question in Parliament revealed that, while 56% of the _____ prisoners under the Unlawful Activities (Prevention) Act (the premier counter-terrorism law) are aged between eighteen and thirty five, the number of such prisoners over sixty is ten. Political prisoners in India thus share the very young demographic profile common to political prisoner the world over, down the ages.

The Bhima-Koregaon Sixteen (BK-16) case however does not follow the same pattern. As of today, all arrested in the case have crossed thirty five, with six in the sixty-plus bracket. Father Stan Swamy, one of the BK-16, passed away in custody when eighty four. Advanced age undoubtedly makes life in prison physically more precarious, but perhaps prepares the mind better. Aside from the unjustness of the arrests, age too, along with the longer track record it carries, has been a factor behind the immense support and solidarity that the case has generated. And there's nothing like solidarity to set the political prisoner's soul free!

From the very beginning, within the first couple of months of the first batch of five arrests on 6th June 2018, Pune's Yerawada Prison was flooded with greetings to the two of them who were crossing their fifty year and sixty year milestones. A baffled prison authority, long unaccustomed to such a show of support, responded with the first weapon they knew – the censor. They refused to give over the cards that came – as if slamming their gate on all the flowers could hold back the spring.

Over the next few months the prisoners struggled for their right to receive support and solidarity and, with backing from beyond the walls, the prison walls, after a while, compelled to relent. Simple messages started coming in and increased even after the case and its prisoners were shifted from Pune to Mumbai. They carried fragrant breezes that drove away the stinky stillnesses that can often envelope a prisoner psyche.

There was nothing that seemed out of the ordinary – not the messages, not the people. A grandmother wrote and mailed a simple card from a rural bylane of Exeter, U.K.; a young man posted on social media from a gully in Delhi. But it is such ordinarinesses that energize the footfalls of history. They silently bored holes through dungeon like barrack walls and brought in the fresh air and light of distant lands.

There were also the statements of those positioned in weighty forums – members of the Lok Sabha and Rajya Sabha, parliamentarians of the E.U., UN rapporteurs and commissioners and commissioners and many more. Solidarity like this has its own impact. It can even nudge out voices of support from the most unexpected quarters.

Such a voice, calling for the release of the incarcerated BK-16, came in the end of July 2022. It was Mr. P. Chidambaram, the Union Home Minister who, during the dying days of December 2008, had piloted the twin Bills that brought the provisions in law that have ensured arrest and lengthy detention of the BK-16 and many other political prisoners. His column, in various languages in leading dailies, precisely red lighted the harsh bail clauses and the sweeping powers of the Central Government to suo motu (on its own motion) take over investigations from a State Government that is not in its camp – these were the very portions that he had bulldozed past the minority in Parliament who had opposed them. He had then promised to, in a few months, revisit and even recall the offending clauses if there seemed to be scope for misuse. His realisation now seems a bit late in the day, but is nevertheless welcome.

However, it is not such Generals that make the difference. It is the Subalterns – the grandmother and the gully boy – who initiate the simple interventions that set into motion the wheels that create history, their wanting and asking for our release in one such intervention. Multiplied a million times over it builds up the winds that augur change.

The BK-16 case is part of such an ongoing experience. A thing we in the case know is that each ordinary act of solidarity reaches us a short step closer to that tipping point which will see all of us out of the prison gates.

But release and individual freedom is rarely an end. Solidarity comes with great expectations, expectations mean great responsibilities – a responsibility to join hands with all those wanting a better world. The BK-16 will have to try and gear up to this responsibility, each in her own way.

One of the lyricists and performers among us sings:

> Your iron bars will melt away
>
> When I sing aloud my songs again
>
> You'll fall you fool just seeing the way
>
> I resolve to join the war again.[3]

*　*　*

8 September 2022
Rupesh Kumar Singh

In service,

Respected President Sir,

Government of India.

Through – jail Superintendent, Mandalkara Seraikela,

Subject – In regards to holding one-day hunger strike in jail on September 13 for provision of basic facilities for the prisoners in jail

---

3.　Translation of a verse from a Marathi song composed in prison by one of the BK16.

and to mark the martyrdom day of great revolutionary immortal martyr Yatindra Nath Das alias Jatin Das.

Mister,

The submission is that I, Rupesh Kumar Singh, father – Arvind Prasad Singh, have been incarcerated as an undertrial prisoner in Jharkhand's Mandalkara Seraikela since July 18, 2022. I am a journalist by profession. As you know that during the British period, a great revolutionary of our country, Jatindra Nath Das alias Jatin Das began a hunger strike on 13 July, 1929, for provision of basic facilities for the then prisoners of Lahore Jail and against the exploitation of prisoners in jail, which lasted for consecutive 62 days till his martyrdom. Therefore, Jatin Das was martyred on 13 September 1929 due to the hunger strike for rights of prisoners.

It has been 75 years since the Britishers left our country. Today our country is celebrating the nectar's festival of independence but even today, the condition of our country's jails is not much better. Today, our country's jails are full of prisoners beyond their capacity. The jails neither have enough constables, nor enough staff. Jail inmates have to do two shifts every day, which is against the 8-hour working day of the Indian labour law. Jail constables do not even get a weekly off.

The worst situation in jail is that of undertrials. Even in small cases, they have to stay in jail without bail for years. Since 18 July, 2022, I have been lodged in Mandalkara Seraikela of Jharkhand, where neither the prisoners get nutritious food and nor do the detained patients get adequate health facilities. Here in a week, puffed dried rice-onion on three days, chickpea-onion on three days, and roasted flattened rice-jaggery on one day is given in breakfast.

Every day, rice, pulse and vegetables for lunch and *rotis*, pulse and vegetable for dinner is given. Yes, two pieces of chicken meat is given on one day in 15 days for posturing.

Is it a nutritious diet for detainees?

Here, incarcerated leprosy patients and incarcerated AIDS patients are caged in cell instead of being kept in hospital. Is this not a violation of the human rights of the incarcerated patients?

Here to call their kin, prisoners have to pay Rs 100 for 40 minutes. Meetings happen one day in 15 days, in which only 10 minutes are permitted for conversation. Is this not financial and mental torture for the prisoners?

Hence, we demand the Respected President Sir that-

1. Proper nutritious food should be provided to the prisoners.

2. Incarcerated patients should be kept in the hospital.

3. Phone facility should be provided to the detainees free of cost.

4. Meetings should be done once a week and at least, 20 minutes should be permitted for conversation.

I would like to tell the Respected President Sir that in support of the above demands, I on 13 September 2022 – on the occasion of the 93rd martyrdom day of the great revolutionary Jatin Das – will go on one-day hunger strike at Mandalkara Seraikela and even then, if proper action is not taken on my aforementioned demands, I will carry forward the revolutionary legacy of the great revolutionary immortal martyr Jatin Das through an indefinite hunger strike.

Hopefully, appropriate action will be taken on my demands.

Applicant

Rupesh Kumar Singh

Undertrial Prisoner,

Seraikela.

The letter was handed over by Rupesh Kumar Singh to jail superintendent on 8 September 2022 to be posted to the President of India.

Translated from Hindi with permission.

* * *

10 October 2022
Hidme Markam

It's good to hear that outside many people are worrying for me or and campaigning for my freedom. In jail i have seen so many people in such difficult circumstances, which has only made me stronger. If any one thinks that I have got scared they are wrong I have only grown stronger and when I come out I will continue fight against injustice. Jail had not defeated me. I have been implicated in a false case but that doesn't make my fight wrong. I was always fighting for justice for my people for my land and will continue do so with all those who do the same. I feel connected to all of you.

7

Name the Names

Date of Arrest (2014–2022)	Name	Sections	Days in Prison	Status
2014				
9 May	G.N. Saibaba	UAPA/IPC 153A/IPC 505(1)(b)/IPC 117/IPC 120B	417	
		Re-arrested on 24 December 2015 after freed on bail on 3 July 2015	99	
		Re-arrested on 7 March 2017 after freed on bail on 1 April	2195	Incarcerated
20 Aug	M. Salman	IPC 124A	33	Released
2 Sep	Bhelke	UAPA	3112	Incarcerated
2 Sep	Kanchan Nanaware	UAPA	2962	Died in Custody
2015				
5 Jan	Jagtar Singh Tara	Explosives Act/Arms Act	3352	Convicted
16 Jan	Somaru Nag	Arms Act	552	Released
29 Jan	Shirin Dalvi	IPC 295A	1	Released
29 Jan	Jaison C. Cooper	UAPA	47	Released
30 Jan	Thushar Nirmal Sarathy	UAPA	48	Released
2 Feb	Santanu Saikia	IPC 457/IPC 380/IPC 420/IPC 468/IPC IPC 471/IPC 120B/IPC 34	80	Released
26 Feb	Surat Singh Khalsa	Preventive charges	60	
		Re-arrested on 1 June 2015 after freed on bail on 27 April 2015	21	

Date of Arrest (2014–2022)	Name	Sections	Days in Prison	Status
2015				
		Re-arrested on 20 July 2015 after freed on bail on 22 June 2015	21	Released
26 Feb	Ravindeer Jeet Singh	Preventive charges	56	Released
26 Feb	Kalimuthu Kanshsamy	IPC 170/IPC 420/ Section 5, Emblems and Names (Prevention of Improper Use) Act 1950	2935	Incarcerated
21 Apr	Rajkumari	IPC 147/IPC 148/ IPC 149/IPC 307/ IPC 343/IPC 333/ IPC 504/IPC 353/ IPC 332/IPC 336/IPC 427/IPC 120b/Section 7, Criminal Act/3 and 5, public property Act/5 and 26, Indian Forest Act	93	Released
4 May	Rupesh	IPC 120(b)/IPC 124A/UAPA	2868	Incarcerated
4 May	Shyna	IPC 120(b)/IPC 124A/UAPA	1198	Released
4 May	Anoop Mathew George	IPC 120(b)/IPC 124A/UAPA	183	Released
4 May	Kannan	IPC 120(b)/IPC 124A/UAPA	2868	Incarcerated
4 May	Veeramani	IPC 120(b)/IPC 124A/UAPA	1940	Released
8 May	Konnath Muralidharan alias Ajith Kannampillai alias Kannakaran	UAPA/Section 164, CrPC/IPC 419/IPC 467/IPC 468/IPC 471/IPC 34	1536	Released
13 May	Ibrahim	UAPA	2409	Released
13 Jun	Masanamuthu	IPC 294B/IPC 353/ IPC 56/UAPA	184	Released

156

Date of Arrest (2014–2022)	Name	Sections	Days in Prison	Status
2015				
13 Jun	Namaman-ickam	IPC 294B/IPC 353/ IPC 56/UAPA	184	Released
29 Sep	Santosh Yadav	UAPA	516	Released
18 Oct	Hardik Patel	IPC 124A/IPC 153A/ IPC 505(2)/IPC 506/ IPC 188/Sedition Act	271	
		Re-arrested on 18 January 2020 after freed on bail on 15 July 2016	5	
		Re-arrested on 23 January 2020 after freed on bail on 23 January 2020	1	
		Re-arrested on 20 March 2020 after freed on bail on 24 January 2020	780	Released
21 Oct	Surinder Singh	Terrorist and Disruptive Activities Act	322	Released
30 Oct	S. Sivadas alias Kovan	Sedition	17	Released
20 Nov	Kishlay Tiwari	Violation of CrPC 144	1	Released
20 Nov	Shubham Vardan	Violation of CrPC 144	1	Released
20 Nov	Ashutosh	Violation of CrPC 144	1	Released
2016				
12 Feb	Kanhaiya Kumar	IPC 124A/IPC 323/ IPC 123/IPC 149/IPC 120B	20	Released
23 Feb	Umar Khalid	UAPA/IPC 120B/ IPC 109/IPC 114/ IPC 124A/IPC 147/ IPC 148/IPC 149/ IPC 153A/IPC 186/ IPC 201/IPC 212/ IPC 295/IPC 302/IPC 307/IPC 341/	23	

Date of Arrest (2014–2022)	Name	Sections	Days in Prison	Status
2016				
	-	IPC 353/IPC 395/ IPC 419/ IPC 420/ IPC 427/IPC 435/ IPC 436/IPC 452/ IPC 454/IPC 468/IPC 471/IPC 34/Section 3 & 4 Prevention of Damage to Public Property Act/Section 25/27 Arms Act/IPC 323/IPC 123		
		Re-arrested on 13 September 2020 after freed on bail on 26 August 2016	909	Incarcerated
23 Feb	Anirban Bhattacharya	IPC 124A/IPC 323/ IPC 123/IPC 149/IPC 120B	23	Released
22 Mar	Prabhat Singh	67 and 67A of the IT Act/IPC 292	96	Released
27 Mar	Deepak Jaiswal	67 and 67A of the IT Act/IPC 292	91	Released
17 Jun	Mahesh Chandra Guru	Hurting religious sentiments	4	Released
19 Jun	Nasir Rangrez	IPC 120B/IPC 121A/ IPC 124A/IPC 153A(1)(b)/IPC 302/ IPC 307/IPC 465/ IPC 471/IPC 212/ Explosives Substances Act/UAPA/Section 27, Arms Act/ Sections 65 and 66, IT Act	2456	Convicted
8 Jul	Piyush Manush	IPC 53/IPC 153/IPC 189/IPC 506(ii)/7 of Criminal Law Amendment Act	13	
		Re-arrested on 18 June 2018 after freed on bail on 21 July 2016	4	Released

Date of Arrest (2014–2022)	Name	Sections	Days in Prison	Status
2016				
25 Dec	Balla Ravin-dranath	Sections 8(1), 8(2), 8(3) and 8(5), Chhattisgarh State Special Public Security Act	187	Released
25 Dec	Duddu Prabhakar	Sections 8(1), 8(2), 8(3) and 8(5), Chhattisgarh State Special Public Security Act	187	Released
25 Dec	Chikkudu Prabhaker	Sections 8(1), 8(2), 8(3) and 8(5), Chhattisgarh State Special Public Security Act	187	Released
25 Dec	Durga Prasad	Sections 8(1), 8(2), 8(3) and 8(5), Chhattisgarh State Special Public Security Act	187	Released
25 Dec	Rajendra Prasad	Sections 8(1), 8(2), 8(3) and 8(5), Chhattisgarh State Special Public Security Act	187	Released
25 Dec	Nazeer	Sections 8(1), 8(2), 8(3) and 8(5), Chhattisgarh State Special Public Security Act	187	Released
25 Dec	Ramanala Laxmaiyya	Sections 8(1), 8(2), 8(3) and 8(5), Chhattisgarh State Special Public Security Act	187	Released
2017				
7 Mar	Pandu Narote	UAPA/IPC 153A/IPC 505(1)(b)/IPC 117/ IPC 120B	1997	Died in Custody
7 Mar	Mahesh Tirki	UAPA/IPC 153A/IPC 505(1)(b)/IPC 117/ IPC 120B	2195	Incarcerated

Date of Arrest (2014–2022)	Name	Sections	Days in Prison	Status
2017				
7 Mar	Vijay Tirki	UAPA/IPC 153A/IPC 505(1)(b)/IPC 117/ IPC 120B	2195	Incarcerated
7 Mar	Prashant Rahi	UAPA/IPC 153A/IPC 505(1)(b)/IPC 117/ IPC 120B	2195	Incarcerated
7 Mar	Hem Mishra	UAPA/IPC 153A/IPC 505(1)(b)/IPC 117/ IPC 120B	2195	Incarcerated
2 Apr	Zakir Ali Tyagi	IPC 124A	42	Released
15 Apr	M. Valamarthi	Goonda Act/IPC 294(b)/IPC 447/ IPC 506(i)/IPC 153/ IPC 505(i)(b)/IPC 53/IPC 506(ii)/7(1) (a) of Criminal Law Amendment Act	35	
		Re-arrested on 12 Jully 2017 after freed on bail on 20 May 2017	57	
		Re-arrested on 19 June 2018 after freed on bail on 7 September 2017	18	Released
29 May	Thirumurugan Gandhi	Goonda Act/IPC 124A/IPC 153A/IPC 153B/IPC 505/UAPA	115	
		Re-arrested on 9 August 2018 after freed on bail on 20 September 2017	55	Released
6 Jun	Kanyakumari	UAPA	2104	Incarcerated
8 Jun	Chandrashek-har Azad Ravan	IPC 325/IPC 436/ IPC 147/IPC 148/ IPC 149/IPC 186/ IPC 323/IPC 332/IPC 353/IPC 151/Section 3 and 4 of PDPP Act	464	
		Re-arrested on 21 December 2019 after freed on bail on 14 September 2018	26	

Date of Arrest (2014–2022)	Name	Sections	Days in Prison	Status
2017				
		Re-arrested on 26 January 2020 after freed on bail on 16 January 2020	1	
		Re-arrested on 1 July 2022 after freed on bail on 26 January 2020	5	Released
30 Jun	Jayaraman	IPC 506/IPC 307/IPC 341/IPC 143/IPC 188	43	
		Re-arrested on 11 December 2017 after freed on bail on 1 August 2017	1	
		Re-arrested on 1 February 2019 after freed on bail on 11 December 2017	47	Released
30 Jun	Dharmaraj	IPC 506/IPC 307	43	Released
30 Jun	Murugan	IPC 506/IPC 307	43	Released
30 Jun	Viduthalai Sudar	IPC 506/IPC 307	43	Released
30 Jun	Santhosh	IPC 506/IPC 307	43	Released
30 Jun	Ramesh	IPC 506/IPC 307	43	Released
30 Jun	Saminathan	IPC 506/IPC 307	43	Released
30 Jun	Silambarasan	IPC 506/IPC 307	43	Released
30 Jun	Senthil Kumar	IPC 506/IPC 307	43	Released
30 Jun	Venkatraman	IPC 506/IPC 307	43	Released
25 Jul	Divya Bharathi	IPC 153A/Section 505(1)(b) and 2 of Prevention of Insults to National Honor Act/Section 66F of Information Technology Act	1	Released
9 Aug	Medha Patkar	IPC 353/IPC 365	15	Released
13 Sep	Tausif Pathan	IPC 120B/IPC 121A/ IPC 124A/IPC 153A(1)(b)/IPC 302/ IPC 307/IPC 465/IPC 471/IPC 212/	2005	Convicted

Date of Arrest (2014–2022)	Name	Sections	Days in Prison	Status
2017				
		Explosives Substances Act/UAPA/Section 27, Arms Act/ Sections 65 and 66, IT Act		
27 Oct	Vinod Verma	Extortion	62	Released
2 Nov	Nakkeeran Pugazhendhi	IPC 142/IPC 146/IPC 294B/IPC 323/IPC 504/IPC 506(1)	3	Released
4 Nov	Jagtar Singh Johal	UAPA/Arms Act	1953	Incarcerated
5 Nov	G. Balakrishnan	IPC 501/Section 67 of the IT Act	1	Released
11 Dec	Chitra	IPC 341/IPC 143/ IPC 188	1	Released
11 Dec	Arulnesan	IPC 341/IPC 143/ IPC 188	1	Released
11 Dec	Prithviraj	IPC 341/IPC 143/ IPC 188	1	Released
16 Dec	Kobad Ghandy	IPC 124A/UAPA	618	
		Re-arrested on 26 August 2019 after being handed over to Gujarat Police	51	Released
26 Dec	Priyanka Borpujari	IPC 353	1	Released
2018				
23 Jan	Abhilash Padacherry	IPC 353	1	Released
23 Jan	Ananthu Rajagopal	IPC 353	1	Released
20 Feb	Upendra Nayak	IPC 121/IPC 121A/ IPC 124A/UAPA	31	Released
15 Mar	Abdul Hannan	IPC 124A	3	Released
26 May	Velmurugan	NSA	23	Released
6 Jun	Sudhir Dhawale	UAPA/IPC 124A/121/121A	1739	Incarcerated
6 Jun	Rona Wilson	UAPA/IPC 153A/IPC 505(1)(B)/IPC 121/ IPC 121A/IPC 124A	1739	Incarcerated

Date of Arrest (2014–2022)	Name	Sections	Days in Prison	Status
2018				
6 Jun	Surendra Gadling	UAPA/IPC 153A/IPC 505(1)(B)/IPC 121/IPC 121A/IPC 124A	1739	Incarcerated
6 Jun	Mahesh Raut	UAPA/IPC 153A/IPC 505(1)(B)/IPC 121/IPC 121A/IPC 124A	1739	Incarcerated
6 Jun	Shoma Sen	UAPA/IPC 153A/IPC 505(1)/IPC 117/IPC 120B	1739	Incarcerated
6 Jun	Jati Anchal Chalwal	UAPA/IPC 153A/IPC 505(1)(b)/IPC 117/IPC 120B	1739	Incarcerated
6 Jun	Sukalo Gond	IPC 147/IPC 148/IPC 149/IPC 307/IPC 343/IPC 333/IPC 504/IPC 353/IPC 332/IPC 336/IPC 427/IPC 120b/Section 7, Criminal Act/3 and 5, public property Act/5 and 26, Indian Forest Act	120	Released
6 Jun	Kismatiya Gond	IPC 147/IPC 148/IPC 149/IPC 307/IPC 343/IPC 333/IPC 504/IPC 353/IPC 332/IPC 336/IPC 427/IPC 120b/Section 7, Criminal Act/3 and 5, public property Act/5 and 26, Indian Forest Act	112	Released
6 Jun	Sukhdev Gond	IPC 147/IPC 148/IPC 149/IPC 307/IPC 343/IPC 333/IPC 504/IPC 353/IPC 332/IPC 336/IPC 427/IPC 120b/Section 7, Criminal Act/3 and 5, public property Act/5 and 26, Indian Forest Act	112	Released
8 Jun	Ishita Singh	IPC 153/IPC 501/IPC 505(1)/IPC 505(2)/IPC 420/IPC 467	11	Released

Date of Arrest (2014–2022)	Name	Sections	Days in Prison	Status
2018				
11 Jun	M. Mahesh Kumar	IPC 147/IPC 148/ IPC 188/IPC 353/ IPC 506(2)/Section 3 of Tamil Nadu Property Prevention of Damage and Loss	50	Released
14 Jun	M. Rajkumar	Sections of PDPP	45	Released
20 Jun	S. Vanchina-than	IPC 147/IPC 148/ IPC 188/IPC 353/ IPC 506(2)/Section 3 of Tamil Nadu Property Prevention of Damage and Loss	16	Released
21 Jun	Hussain Khan	IPC 353	4	Released
22 Jun	Ram Parmar	IPC 353	4	Released
31 Jul	Satish Uke	IPC 120B/IPC 420/ IPC 423/IPC 424/ IPC 447/IPC 465/ IPC 467/IPC 468/IPC 471/IPC 474/Section 3, PMLA	10	Released
		Re-arrested on 31 March 2022 after freed on bail on 10 August 2018	335	Incarcerated
8 Aug	Neta Nag	IPC 124A	1406	Released
28 Aug	Sudha Bharadwaj	UAPA/IPC 153A/IPC 505(1)/IPC 120B/IPC 117/IPC 34/IPC 121/ IPC 121A/IPC 124A	1199	Released
28 Aug	Arun Ferreira	UAPA/IPC 153A/IPC 505(1)/IPC 120B/IPC 117/IPC 34/IPC 121/ IPC 121A/IPC 124A	1676	Incarcerated
28 Aug	Vernon Gonsalves	UAPA/IPC 153A/IPC 505(1)/IPC 120B/IPC 117/IPC 34/IPC 121/ IPC 121A/IPC 124A	1676	Incarcerated
28 Aug	Varavara Rao	UAPA/IPC 153A/IPC 505(1)/IPC 120B/IPC 117/IPC 34/IPC 121/ IPC 121A/IPC 124A	921	Released

Date of Arrest (2014–2022)	Name	Sections	Days in Prison	Status
2018				
30 Aug	Gautam Navlakha	UAPA/IPC 153A/IPC 505(1)/IPC 120B/IPC 117/IPC 34/IPC 121/ IPC 121A/IPC 124A	31	
		Re-arrested on 14 April 2020 after freed on bail on 1 October 2018	1061	Incarcerated
3 Sep	Lois Sofia	IPC 505/IPC 290/75(I)(c) of the Tamil Nadu City Police Act	1	Released
6 Oct	Danish	UAPA	1617	Incarcerated
9 Oct	RR Gopal	IPC 124A	1	Released
10 Oct	Karam Singh Munda	IPC 124A	1612	Released
23 Oct	Abhijit Iyer Mitra	IPC 294/IPC 295A/ IPC 506/IPC 500/IPC 153A/Section 67 of IT Act	43	Released
		Re-arrested on 24 April 2022 after freed on bail on 1 October 2018	321	Incarcerated
2019				
19 Mar	Samiul Biswas	IPC 379	15	Released
25 May	Jeetrai Handsa	IPC 153A/IPC 295A/ IPC 505	13	Released
8 Jun	Prashant Kanoija	IPC 500/IPC 505/ Section 67 of the IT Act	3	
		Re-arrested on 18 August 2020 after freed on bail on 12 June 2019	78	Released
9 Jun	Santosh Jaiswal	IPC 388/IPC 186	6	Released
8 Sep	Anuj Shukla	IPC 153/IPC 501/IPC 505(1)/IPC 505(2)/ IPC 420/IPC 467	44	Released
11 Sep	Dinesh Kumar	IPC 147/IPC 332/ IPC 353/IPC 504/IPC 506/IPC 186	1	Released

Date of Arrest (2014–2022)	Name	Sections	Days in Prison	Status
2019				
1 Nov	Alan Shuhaib	UAPA/IPC 120B/	315	Released
1 Nov	Thwaha Fasal	UAPA/IPC 120B	614	Released
6 Nov	Anshul Kaushik	IPC 153/IPC 501/IPC 505(1)/IPC 505(2)/ IPC 420/IPC 467	41	Released
6 Nov	Amit Sharma	Illegal detention	1	Released
12 Nov	N. Ravi Sharma	UAPA/IPC 120B/ IPC 34/Section 8(1) (2), Telangana State Public Security Act	1215	Incarcerated
12 Nov	Anuradha	UAPA/IPC 120B/ IPC 34/Section 8(1) (2), Telangana State Public Security Act	1215	Incarcerated
19 Dec	Mohammad Shuaib	IPC 147/IPC 148/ IPC 152/IPC 307/ IPC 323/IPC 506/ IPC 332/IPC 353/IPC 188/IPC 435/PDPP	33	Released
19 Dec	Sadaf Jafar	IPC 147/IPC 148/ IPC 152/IPC 307/ IPC 323/IPC 506/ IPC 332/IPC 353/IPC 188/IPC 435/PDPP	20	Released
20 Dec	Shameem Abbas	PDPP 3/PDPP 4/IPC 147/IPC 148/IPC 149/ IPC 307/IPC 332/IPC 333/IPC 336/IPC 427/ IPC 436/IPC 353/IPC 323/IPC 188/IPC 341/	16	Released
20 Dec	Qummail Abbas	PDPP 3/PDPP 4/IPC 147/IPC 148/IPC 149/ IPC 307/IPC 332/IPC 333/IPC 336/IPC 427/ IPC 436/IPC 353/IPC 323/IPC 188/IPC 341/	16	Released
20 Dec	Deepak Kabir	PDPP 3/PDPP 4/IPC 147/IPC 148/IPC 149/ IPC 307/IPC 332/IPC 333/IPC 336/IPC 427/ IPC 436/IPC 353/IPC 323/IPC 188/IPC 341/	21	Released

Date of Arrest (2014–2022)	Name	Sections	Days in Prison	Status
2019				
23 Dec	Mohammad Faisal	IPC 145/IPC 149/IPC 153A/IPC 505	16	Released
2020				
4 Jan	Meeran Haider	IPC 124A/IPC 302/ IPC 307/IPC 153A/ IPC 120B	1162	Incarcerated
8 Jan	Nalini Balakumar	IPC 124A/IPC 34	3	Released
18 Jan	C. Kaseem	IPC 124A/UAPA	123	Released
28 Jan	Sharjeel Imam	IPC 124A/IPC 153A/ IPC 153B/IPC 505/ UAPA	1138	Incarcerated
30 Jan	Kafeel Khan	153A/NSA	263	Released
30 Jan	Farida Begum	IPC 124A	8	Released
30 Jan	Najibunissa	IPC 124A	8	Released
17 Feb	Sandeep Pandey	IPC 151	1	Released
19 Feb	Rajabaxi H V	IPC 505	1	Released
19 Feb	Siraj Bisaralli	IPC 505	1	Released
19 Feb	R Suresh	IPC 120(B)/IPC 188/ IPC 121/IPC 121A/ UAPA	1116	Incarcerated
20 Feb	Amulya Leona	IPC 124A/UAPA	111	Released
26 Feb	Sabu Ansari	IPC 147/IPC 148/ IPC 149/IPC 186/ IPC 307/IPC 332/IPC 353/IPC 109/IPC 34/ Section 25 and 27 of Arms Act	63	Released
26 Feb	Khalid Saifi	UAPA/IPC 120B/ IPC 109/IPC 114/ IPC 124A/IPC 147/ IPC 148/IPC 149/ IPC 153A/IPC 186/ IPC 188/IPC 201/ IPC 212/IPC 283/ IPC 295/IPC 302/ IPC 307/IPC 323/ IPC 341/IPC 332/ IPC 353/IPC 395/IPC 419/ IPC 420/IPC 427/IPC 435/	1109	Incarcerated

Date of Arrest (2014–2022)	Name	Sections	Days in Prison	Status
2020				
26 Feb	Ishrat Jahan	IPC 436/IPC 452/ IPC 454/IPC 468/ IPC 471/IPC 505/ IPC 34/Section 3 & 4 Prevention of Damage to Public Property Act/Section 25/27 Arms Act UAPA/IPC 120B/ IPC 109/IPC 114/ IPC 124A/IPC 147/ IPC 148/IPC 149/ IPC 153A/IPC 186/ IPC 201/IPC 212/IPC 295/IPC 302/IPC 307/ IPC 332/IPC 341/IPC 353/IPC 395/IPC 419/ IPC 420/IPC 427/IPC 435/IPC 436/IPC 452/ IPC 454/IPC 468/IPC 471/IPC 34/Section 3 & 4 Prevention of Damage to Public Property Act/Section 25/27 Arms Act	747	Released
3 Mar	Shahrukh Pathan	UAPA/IPC 120B/ IPC 109/IPC 114/ IPC 124A/IPC 147/ IPC 148/IPC 149/ IPC 153A/IPC 186/ IPC 188/IPC 201/IPC 212/IPC 216/IPC 295/ IPC 302/IPC 307/IPC 341/IPC 353/IPC 395/ IPC 419/ IPC 420/ IPC 427/IPC 435/ IPC 436/IPC 452/ IPC 454/IPC 468/IPC 471/IPC 34/Section 3 & 4 Prevention of Damage to Public Property Act/Section 25/27 Arms Act	1103	Incarcerated

168

Date of Arrest (2014–2022)	Name	Sections	Days in Prison	Status
2020				
9 Mar	Mohd Danish	Section 3, 70 and 4 PMLA	4	Released
9 Mar	Parvez Alam	Section 3, 70 and 4 PMLA	4	Released
9 Mar	Mohammad Ilyas	Section 3, 70 and 4 PMLA	4	Released
11 Mar	Mohd. Saleem Khan	IPC 332/IPC 323/ UAPA/IPC 120B/ IPC 109/IPC 114/ IPC 124A/IPC 147/ IPC 148/IPC 149/IPC 153A/IPC 186/IPC 201/IPC 212/IPC 295/ IPC 302/IPC 307/IPC 341/IPC 353/IPC 395/ IPC 419/ IPC 420/ IPC 427/IPC 435/ IPC 436/IPC 452/ IPC 454/IPC 468/IPC 471/IPC 34/Section 3 & 4 Prevention of Damage to Public Property Act/Section 25/27 Arms Act	1095	Incarcerated
3 Apr	Firoz Khan	UAPA/IPC 147/ IPC 148/IPC 149/ IPC 427/IPC 436/ IPC 121A/IPC 120B/ Explosives Substances Act/Arms Act	56	
		Re-arrested on 16 February 2021 after freed on bail on 29 May 2020	752	Incarcerated
6 Apr	Shadab Ahmed	UAPA/IPC 120B/IPC 332/IPC 109/IPC 114/ IPC 124A/IPC 147/ IPC 148/IPC 149/IPC 153A/IPC 186/IPC 201/IPC 212/IPC 295/ IPC 302/IPC 307/IPC 341/IPC 353/	1069	Incarcerated

Date of Arrest (2014–2022)	Name	Sections	Days in Prison	Status
2020				
		IPC 395/IPC 419/ IPC 420/IPC 427/ IPC 435/IPC 436/ IPC 452/IPC 454/ IPC 468/IPC 471/ IPC 34/Section 3 & 4 Prevention of Damage to Public Property Act/Section 25/27 Arms Act		
7 Apr	Damodharan	IPC 188/IPC 505(1) (b)	10	Released
10 Apr	Safoora Zargar	IPC 147/IPC 148/ IPC 149/IPC 120B/ IPC 302/IPC 307/ IPC 124A/IPC 153A/ IPC 186/IPC 253/ IPC 395/IPC 427/ IPC 435/IPC 436/ IPC 454/IPC 109/IPC 114/3 and 4 PDPP Act/13, 16, 17 and 18 UAPA	76	Released
14 Apr	Rahul Kulkarni	IPC 269/IPC 270/ IPC 505(b)/IPC 188/ IPC 117/ Section 3, Epidemic Diseases Act	2	Released
14 Apr	Anand Teltumbde	UAPA/IPC 153A/IPC 505(1)/IPC 120B/IPC 117/IPC 34/IPC 121/ IPC 121A/IPC 124A	1061	Incarcerated
16 Apr	Amir Mintoee	IPC 332/IPC 353/ IPC 395/Violation of CPC 144	95	Released
23 Apr	Andrew Sam Raja Pandian	IPC 188/IPC 505(1) (b)	1	Released
26 Apr	Shifa Ur Rehman	UAPA/IPC 120B/ IPC 109/IPC 114/ IPC 124A/IPC 147/ IPC 148/IPC 149/IPC 153A/IPC 186/IPC 201/IPC 212/	1049	Incarcerated

Date of Arrest (2014–2022)	Name	Sections	Days in Prison	Status
2020				
27 Apr	Zubair Ahmed	IPC 295/IPC 302/ IPC 307/IPC 341/ IPC 353/IPC 395/ IPC 419/ IPC 420/ IPC 427/IPC 435/ IPC 436/IPC 452/ IPC 454/IPC 468/IPC 471/IPC 34/Section 3 & 4 Prevention of Damage to Public Property Act/Section 25/27 Arms Act Section 51 of the Disaster Management Act/IPC 188/IPC 269/IPC 270/IPC 505(1)(b)	1	Released
28 Apr	Tasleem Ahmed	UAPA/IPC 120B/ IPC 109/IPC 114/ IPC 124A/IPC 147/ IPC 148/IPC 149/ IPC 153A/IPC 186/ IPC 188/IPC 201/ IPC 212/IPC 283/ IPC 295/IPC 302/ IPC 307/IPC 341/ IPC 353/IPC 395/ IPC 419/ IPC 420/ IPC 427/IPC 435/ IPC 436/IPC 452/ IPC 454/IPC 468/IPC 471/IPC 34/Section 3 & 4 Prevention of Damage to Public Property Act/Section 25/27 Arms Act	1047	Incarcerated
3 May	Tahir Hussain	IPC 120/IPC 147/ IPC 148/IPC 149/ IPC 427/IPC 435/IPC 436/IPC 395	1042	Incarcerated
11 May	Dhaval Patel	IPC 124A	15	Released

171

Date of Arrest (2014–2022)	Name	Sections	Days in Prison	Status
2020 17 May	Asif Tanha Iqbal	IPC 147/IPC 148/ IPC 149/IPC 120B/ IPC 109/IPC 114/ IPC 124A/IPC 153A/ IPC 186/IPC 201/ IPC 212/IPC 295/ IPC 302/IPC 307/ IPC 341/IPC 353/ IPC 395/IPC 419/ IPC 427/IPC 435/ IPC 436/IPC 454/IPC 468/IPC 471/IPC 34/ IPC 143/IPC 323/IPC 186/ IPC 332/IPC 308/IPC 120B/3 and 4 PDPP Act/13, 16, 17 and 18 UAPA	397	Released
23 May	Natasha Narwal	UAPA/IPC 120B/ IPC 109/IPC 114/ IPC 124A/IPC 147/ IPC 148/IPC 149/ IPC 153A/IPC 186/ IPC 188/IPC 201/ IPC 212/IPC 283/ IPC 295/IPC 302/ IPC 307/IPC 323/ IPC 341/IPC 332/ IPC 353/IPC 395/ IPC 419/ IPC 420/ IPC 427/IPC 435/ IPC 436/IPC 452/ IPC 454/IPC 468/IPC 471/IPC 34/Section 3 & 4 Prevention of Damage to Public Property Act/Section 25/27 Arms Act	390	Released
24 May	Devangana Kalita	UAPA/IPC 120B/ IPC 109/IPC 114/ IPC 124A/IPC 147/ IPC 148/IPC 149/ IPC 153A/IPC 186/ IPC 188/IPC 201/IPC 212/IPC 283/	389	Released

Date of Arrest (2014–2022)	Name	Sections	Days in Prison	Status
2020				
		IPC 295/IPC 302/ IPC 307/IPC 323/ IPC 341/IPC 332/ IPC 353/IPC 395/ IPC 419/ IPC 420/ IPC 427/IPC 435/ IPC 436/IPC 452/ IPC 454/IPC 468/IPC 471/IPC 34/Section 3 & 4 Prevention of Damage to Public Property Act/Section 25/27 Arms Act		
28 May	Ravish Ali Khan	IPC 332/IPC 353/ IPC 395/Violation of CPC 144	1	Released
28 May	Farhan Zuberi	IPC 332/IPC 353/ IPC 395/Violation of CPC 144	100	Released
1 Jun	Abdulhaque	IPC 307/IPC 333/ IPC 337/IPC 143/ IPC 145/IPC 147/ IPC 151/IPC 152/ IPC 153/IPC 188/IPC 120B	66	Released
3 Jun	Gulfisha Fatima	IPC 147/IPC 148/ IPC 149/IPC 120B/ IPC 302/IPC 307/ IPC 124A/IPC 153A/ IPC 186/IPC 253/ IPC 395/IPC 427/ IPC 435/IPC 436/ IPC 454/IPC 109/IPC 114/3 and 4 PDPP Act/13, 16, 17 and 18 UAPA	1011	Incarcerated
16 Jun	Mohinder Pal Singh	Sections 13, 16, 18 and 20 of UAPA/ Sections 25, 54 and 59 of Arms Act	998	Incarcerated

Date of Arrest (2014–2022)	Name	Sections	Days in Prison	Status
2020				
18 Jun	Lovepreet Singh	Sections 13, 16, 18 and 20 of UAPA/ Sections 25, 54 and 59 of Arms Act	996	Incarcerated
23 Jun	Gurtej Singh	Sections 13, 16, 18 and 20 of UAPA/ Sections 25, 54 and 59 of Arms Act	991	Incarcerated
25 Jun	Salim Malik	UAPA/IPC 120B/ IPC 109/IPC 114/ IPC 124A/IPC 147/ IPC 148/IPC 149/ IPC 153A/IPC 186/ IPC 201/IPC 212/ IPC 295/IPC 302/ IPC 307/IPC 341/ IPC 353/IPC 395/ IPC 419/ IPC 420/ IPC 423/IPC 427/ IPC 435/IPC 436/ IPC 452/IPC 454/ IPC 468/IPC 471/ IPC 34/Section 3 & 4 Prevention of Damage to Public Property Act/Section 25/27 Arms Act	989	Incarcerated
26 Jun	Sukhchain Singh	Sections 13, 16, 18 and 20 of UAPA/ Sections 25, 54 and 59 of Arms Act	168	Released
28 Jun	Jaspreet Singh	Sections 13, 16, 18 and 20 of UAPA/ Sections 25, 54 and 59 of Arms Act	15	Released
29 Jun	Amritpal Singh	Sections 13, 16, 18 and 20 of UAPA/ Sections 25, 54 and 59 of Arms Act	169	Released

Date of Arrest (2014–2022)	Name	Sections	Days in Prison	Status
2020				
2 Jul	Athar Khan	IPC 332/IPC 144/ UAPA/IPC 120B/ IPC 109/IPC 114/ IPC 124A/IPC 147/ IPC 148/IPC 149/ IPC 153A/IPC 186/ IPC 201/IPC 212/IPC 295/IPC 302/ IPC 307/IPC 341/ IPC 353/IPC 395/ IPC 419/ IPC 420/ IPC 427/IPC 435/ IPC 436/IPC 452/ IPC 454/IPC 468/IPC 471/IPC 34/Section 3 & 4 Prevention of Damage to Public Property Act/Section 25/27 Arms Act	982	Incarcerated
8 Jul	Sharjeel Usmani	IPC 307/IPC 147/ IPC 148/IPC 149/ IPC 153/IPC 188/ IPC 189/IPC 332/ IPC 336/IPC 504/ IPC 506/Section 7, Criminal Law Amendment Act/ Section 3, Prevention of Damage to Public Property Act	56	Released
10 Jul	Joginder Singh Gujjar	UAPA	28	Released
24 Jul	Babita Kachchap	IPC 121A/IPC 124A/ IPC 153A	375	Released
28 Jul	Hany Babu	UAPA/IPC 153A/IPC 505(1)/IPC 120B/IPC 117/IPC 34/IPC 121/ IPC 121A/IPC 124A	957	Incarcerated

Date of Arrest (2014–2022)	Name	Sections	Days in Prison	Status
2020				
29 Jul	Faizan Khan	UAPA/IPC 120B/ IPC 109/IPC 114/ IPC 124A/IPC 147/ IPC 148/IPC 149/ IPC 153A/IPC 186/ IPC 201/IPC 212/ IPC 295/IPC 302/ IPC 307/IPC 341/ IPC 353/IPC 395/ IPC 419/ IPC 420/ IPC 427/IPC 435/IPC 436/IPC 452/ IPC 454/IPC 468/IPC 471/IPC 34/Section 3 & 4 Prevention of Damage to Public Property Act/Section 25/27 Arms Act	87	Released
31 Jul	Umesh Kumar Sharma	IPC 420/IPC 467/ IPC 468/IPC 469/IPC 471/IPC 120B	35	Released
11 Aug	Bilal Saifi	IPC 147/IPC 148/ IPC 149/IPC 186/ IPC 307/IPC 332/IPC 353/IPC 109/IPC 34/ Section 25 and 27 of Arms Act	85	Released
7 Sep	Ramesh Gaichor	UAPA/IPC 153A/IPC 505(1)(B)/IPC 121/ IPC 121A/IPC 124A	915	Incarcerated
7 Sep	Sagar Gorkhe	UAPA/IPC 153A/IPC 505(1)/IPC 120B/IPC 117/IPC 34/IPC 121/ IPC 121A/IPC 124A	915	Incarcerated
8 Sep	Jyoti Jagtap	UAPA/IPC 153A/IPC 505(1)/IPC 120B/IPC 117/IPC 34/IPC 121/ IPC 121A/IPC 124A	767	Incarcerated
14 Sep	Rajeev Sharma	Official Secrets Act	81	Released

Date of Arrest (2014–2022)	Name	Sections	Days in Prison	Status
2020				
29 Sep	Salman Patel	IPC 307/IPC 333/ IPC 337/IPC 143/ IPC 145/IPC 147/ IPC 151/IPC 152/ IPC 153/IPC 188/IPC 120B	157	Released
5 Oct	Siddique Kappan	UAPA/IPC 124A/ IPC 153A/IPC 295A/ IPC 120B/Section of IT Act	850	Released
5 Oct	Atikur Rahman	UAPA/IPC 124A/ IPC 153A/IPC 295A/ IPC 120B/Section of IT Act	887	Incarcerated
5 Oct	Masood Ahmad	UAPA/IPC 124A/ IPC 153A/IPC 295A/ IPC 120B/Section of IT Act	887	Incarcerated
5 Oct	Mohammad Alam	UAPA/IPC 124A/ IPC 153A/IPC 295A/ IPC 120B/Section of IT Act	322	Released
8 Oct	Fr. Stan Swamy	UAPA/IPC 153A/IPC 505(1)/IPC 120B/IPC 117/IPC 34/IPC 121/ IPC 121A/IPC 124A	674	Died in Custody
18 Oct	Ahan Penkar	IPC 188/IPC 120B/ IPC 269/IPC 270/ Section 3, Epidemic Act	1	Released
2 Nov	Pradeepika Saraswat	IPC 151	6	Released
5 Nov	Jagtar Singh Hawara	Explosives Act/Arms Act	856	Convicted
16 Nov	Rajeevan	Arms Act/UAPA	845	Incarcerated
23 Nov	Pangi Naganna	UAPA/IPC 124A	838	Incarcerated
5 Dec	Abdullah Danish	Sedition	826	Incarcerated
9 Dec	Rajan	Arms Act/UAPA	822	Incarcerated
12 Dec	Rauf Sharif	PMLA	819	Incarcerated
15 Dec	Andaluri Annapurna	UAPA/IPC 124A	816	Incarcerated

Date of Arrest (2014–2022)	Name	Sections	Days in Prison	Status
2020				
24 Dec	Bopuddi Anjamma	UAPA/IPC 124A	807	Incarcerated
24 Dec	Rela Rajeswari	UAPA/IPC 124A	807	Incarcerated
2021				
1 Jan	Munawar Faruqi	IPC 295A/IPC 269	37	Released
1 Jan	Edvin Anthony	IPC 295A/IPC 269	44	Released
1 Jan	Prakhar Vyas	IPC 295A/IPC 269	44	Released
1 Jan	Nalin Yadav	IPC 295A/IPC 269	57	Released
2 Jan	Sadakat Khan	IPC 295A/IPC 269	58	Released
11 Jan	Harshali Potdar	IPC 153A	1	Released
12 Jan	Nodeep Kaur	ICP 148/ICP 149/ ICP 186/ICP 332/ ICP 352/ICP 353, ICP 384/ICP 379B/ ICP 307	47	Released
21 Jan	Vijith Vijayan	UAPA	779	Incarcerated
23 Jan	Shiv Kumar	ICP 148/ICP 149/ ICP 186/ICP 332/ ICP 352/ICP 353, ICP 384/ICP 379B/ ICP 307	45	Released
30 Jan	Mandeep Punia	IPC 186/IPC 332/IPC 353/IPC 34	4	Released
4 Feb	Dinesh	IPC 341/IPC 294(b)/ IPC 323/IPC 324/IPC 326/IPC 34	40	Released
15 Feb	Disha Ravi	IPC 124A	5	Released
16 Feb	Ansad Badruddin	IPC 121A/IPC 120B/ UAPA/Explosives Substances Act/Arms Act	753	Incarcerated
9 Mar	Hidme Markam	UAPA/IPC 147/IPC 148/IPC 149/IPC 307/ IPC 120B/IPC 363/ IPC 364/IPC 366/IPC 302/IPC 342/25 and 27 of Arms Act/	732	Incarcerated
16 Mar	Anuj Singh Yadav	IPC 124A	81	Released

Date of Arrest (2014–2022)	Name	Sections	Days in Prison	Status
2021				
7 Apr	Laishram Herojit Singh	UAPA	5	Released
7 May	Aslam Khan	IPC 124A	57	Released
7 May	Atiq	IPC 124A	57	Released
7 May	Farid	IPC 124A	57	Released
7 May	Arif	IPC 124A	57	Released
14 May	Raghu Rama Krishna Raju	IPC 124A	8	Released
3 Jun	Raghu Ramakrishnan	IPC 146/IPC 147/ IPC 148/IPC 332/IPC 333/IPC 149	646	Incarcerated
22 Jul	Tanveer Warsi	IPC 177/IPC 186/ IPC 269/IPC 304/ IPC 336/IPC 369/ IPC 417/IPC 34/IPC 120B/Section 12 13 14 & 15 of Press and Book Registration Act, 1867	140	Released
25 Aug	Srishti Jatav	Undisclosed	1	Released
14 Sep	Usman Melethil	UAPA	543	Incarcerated
25 Sep	Naseema	IPC 419/IPC 420/IPC 467/IPC 468/IPC 471	36	Released
25 Sep	Muhsina	IPC 419/IPC 420/IPC 467/IPC 468/IPC 471	36	Released
25 Sep	Haleema	IPC 419/IPC 420/IPC 467/IPC 468/IPC 471	36	Released
13 Nov	Prashant Bose	UAPA/IPC 420/ IPC 467/IPC 468/ IPC 471/Section 17 Criminal Law	483	Incarcerated
13 Nov	Sheela Marandi	UAPA/IPC 420/ IPC 467/IPC 468/ IPC 471/Section 17 Criminal Law	483	Incarcerated
2022				
14 Jan	Narendra Mohanty	IPC 148/IPC 325/IPC 354/IPC186/Section 7, Criminal Law/ Section 4, PDPP	421	Incarcerated

Date of Arrest (2014–2022)	Name	Sections	Days in Prison	Status
2022				
14 Jan	Debendra Swain	IPC 148/IPC 325/IPC 354/IPC186/Section 7, Criminal Law/ Section 4, PDPP	421	Incarcerated
14 Jan	Murlidhar Sahoo	IPC 148/IPC 325/IPC 354/IPC186/Section 7, Criminal Law/ Section 4, PDPP	421	Incarcerated
15 Mar	Gaurav Bansal	IPC 147/IPC 149/ IPC 323/IPC 353/IPC 504/7, Criminal Law Amendment.	7	Released
31 Mar	Pradip Uke	Section 3, PMLA	345	Incarcerated
4 Apr	Sharif Parvaz	IPC 505/IPC 153/ IPC 298	341	Incarcerated
24 Apr	Arkadeep Goswami	IPC 149/IPC 124A/ IPC 148/IPC 149/ IPC 120B/IPC 121/ IPC 121A/IPC 122/ IPC 123	321	Incarcerated
25 Apr	Rainu Oyam	Arms Act	320	Incarcerated
20 May	Ratan Lal	IPC 153A/IPC 295A	1	Released
29 May	Abdur Rehman	IPC 295A	2	Released
3 Jun	Zafar Hayat Hashmi	NSA	281	Incarcerated
5 Jun	Sharik Ahmad	IPC 505/IPC 507/IT	60	Released
7 Jun	Roddur Roy	IPC 120(B)/IPC 153/ IPC 153A/IPC 153B/ IPC 189/IPC 417/ IPC 465/IPC 467/ IPC 468/IPC 469/ IPC 500/IPC 501/IPC 504/IPC 505/IPC 505 (1B)/IPC 509	21	Released
11 Jun	Javed Mohammad	NSA	273	Incarcerated
14 Jun	Afsar Alam	IPC 147/IPC 148/ IPC 149/IPC 341/IPC 295A/IPC 153A/IPC 504/IPC 120B	270	Incarcerated

Date of Arrest (2014–2022)	Name	Sections	Days in Prison	Status
2022				
18 Jun	Amir Hamza	IPC 353	266	Incarcerated
22 Jun	Mukhtar Baba	IPC 120B/Uttar Pradesh Gangsters Act	262	Incarcerated
25 Jun	R.B. Sreekumar	IPC 468/IPC 471/ IPC 194/IPC 211/IPC 218/IPC 120B	259	Incarcerated
26 Jun	Teesta Setalvad	IPC 468/IPC 471/ IPC 194/IPC 211/IPC 218/IPC 120B	69	Released
27 Jun	Mohammed Zubair	IPC 153/IPC 153A/ IPC 295A/IPC 505/ IPC 120B/IPC 34	23	Released
5 Jul	Haji Mohammad Wasi	Uttar Pradesh Gansters Act/ Anti-social Activities Prevention Act/NSA	249	Incarcerated
12 Jul	Sanjiv Bhatt	IPC 468/IPC 471/ IPC 194/IPC 211/ IPC 218/IPC 120B Re-arrested from prison	242	Incarcerated
15 Jul	P. Gopi	Telangana Public Security Act/UAPA	239	Incarcerated
17 Jul	Rupesh Kumar Singh	UAPA	237	Incarcerated
29 Sep	Mohd Zaid	UAPA	163	Incarcerated
30 Sep	Abdullah Saood Ansari	IPC 153A/IPC 153B/ UAPA	162	Incarcerated
4 Oct	Asgar Jamali	IPC 120B/IPC 153A/ UAPA	158	Incarcerated
4 Oct	Israr Ali Khan	IPC 120B/IPC 153A/ UAPA	158	Incarcerated
5 Oct	Masud Ahmad	IPC 124A/UAPA	157	Incarcerated
13 Nov	Maulana Irfan Daulat Nadvi	IPC 120/IPC 121A/ IPC 153A/UAPA	118	Incarcerated
3 Mar	Kamal K.P.	IPC153A/IPC295A/ IPC 120B/IT Act/ UAPA	8	Incarcerated

Epilogue:
When the State Enters Your Home[1]

On Friday 10 June 2022, the Muslim community across India took to the streets in large numbers to demand action against Nupur Sharma and Naveen Jindal – respectively, the former BJP spokesperson and the former head of the Delhi BJP's media unit – for their derogatory remarks against Prophet Mohammad. While both party leaders were characterised as 'fringe elements' and suspended from the BJP, no legal action was taken against them. Sharma's insults are not new: BJP members, including Prime Minister Narendra Modi, have often targeted, vilified, spread disinformation and used hate speech to unleash violence against the Muslim community.

As protests grew in intensity especially in Northern India so did the response of the police that intervened against protestors using disproportionate and unjustified violence: what authorities defined as 'mob control' ended with two youths – 14-year-old Mudasir and 19-year-old Sahil Ansari – killed by the police that shot live ammunition against the protesting crowd.[2]

With senior officers cheering at the spectacle, the authorities yet again used democratic protests as an opportunity to further crack down on dissent. Scores of activists and political dissidents were picked up under false charges along with young Muslim boys.[3] To date we do not know the exact number of people who were picked up in these combing operations. Among those named as 'key conspirators' were Welfare Party leader Javed Mohammad, his wife Parveen and daughter Sumaiya (19), who are the parents

---

1. A part of this chapter was published by The Polis Project on 21 June 2022. Francesca Recchia and Suchitra Vijayan, 'Who do we call when the police murders? Fear grows as the Indian Muslim community is under constant attack.'
2. Zafar Aafaq, 'India police crack down on protests against Prophet remarks.' *Al Jazeera*, 11 June 2022.
3. Sumedha Pal, 'Prayagraj protests: "being framed", say anti-CAA protesters as police name them "key conspirators".' *The Wire*, 11 June 2022.

and younger sister of scholar and activist Afreen Fatima, a student leader from Aligarh Muslim University and the JNU, who was the national secretary of the Fraternity Movement. Afreen is a researcher at The Polis Project and her contribution has been instrumental in the making of this book.

In a video message published by Maktoob Media, Afreen described how the police arrested her family members in the middle of the night without being in possession of any warrant or legal notice and, when she and her sister-in-law refused to follow the policemen to the police station, the police threatened to take them by force. The police further threatened to evict them and raze their house to the ground. On the evening of 11 June, they were issued a notice to such effect for the following day and residents were asked to empty their houses to allow them to proceed with the demolition.[4] The authorities, accompanied by a large number of police personnel in riot gear, destroyed Afreen Fatima's home in the early afternoon of 12 June even though many elements of the legal notice proved to be either false or factually wrong.[5] In an act of grotesque cruelty, Afreen's mother and sister were released from custody and the police then drove them to the site so they could be present and watch their house being bulldozed to the ground. At the time of writing, Javed Mohammad remains in jail and Afreen Fatima is in a safe location after being moved multiple times as there are realistic fears that she may be falsely implicated by the state in various open FIRs in fabricated conspiracy cases or worse targeted with extrajudicial violence.

The days that precede and follow the destruction of Afreen's house remain for us a blur. We sent 218 emails to journalists, civil society activists, elected leaders and many others to make sure the news of her persecution would not disappear and be drawn in indifference. Those are foggy, sleepless nights and days in which

---

4. The Polis Project obtained from the family a copy of the notice and published it on their Twitter account on 11 June 2022. See https://twitter.com/project_polis/status/1535683423356047360?s=20&t=wbOrhhx9Rbx1Pj026G7vcg.

5. In concertation with the legal council of the family, The Polis Project reconstructed the evidence of the false and factually wrong allegations by the police. See https://twitter.com/project_polis/status/1535951492548550657?s=20&t=KTnoX24pgpAEOVXKvmrDXg.

we tried all we could to ensure her a margin of safety while reckoning at a personal level with the monstrosity of the Indian state.

Weeks later, Sahba Husain – who is Gautam Navlakha's partner and a scholar who has extensively worked on state violence in Indian occupied Kashmir – told us that there is no amount of studying and dealing with violence that would ever prepare you for the moment in which the state enters your home. In retrospect, those words now ring tremendously true.

Nothing can ever prepare you to deal with the fact that your loved ones are under attack while you try to disentangle yourself from the claws of suspicion, fear and paranoia.

After the dust of the destruction of Afreen's house settled, we came to realise that besides her mother's cherished plants, her books, clothes and her favourite stationery box, also her laptop and notebooks were lost in the rubble – and with them, a good chunk of the material that was meant to be part of this book. While in the overwhelming sense of loss the unspoken temptation of giving this project up crossed our minds, what became crystal clear – and in its own very special way gave us strength – was the fact that this book had become itself part of the story we were trying to tell.

This is the story of a cruel state, that is intolerant of any form of resistance, deploys unmitigated violence and goes above and beyond to eradicate dissent at its very roots. This is the story of a vindictive state that, in utter disregard of its Constitution and international laws, uses collective punishment and wages a systematic war against its own citizens to silence and eliminate its opponents.

The book is not just a list of atrocities, it tells a story about how the Indian state is stripping its citizens of their rights and has robbed thousands of their dignity before it robs them of their humanity.

In ways we had neither planned nor expected, this book has become an act of intellectual, ethical and moral resistance as it is an act of community and solidarity.

As we travelled across India, we were regularly asked two questions: Are you not afraid? Aren't you under surveillance? One thing became clear when we met prisoners (a lucky few now out on bail), families, friends, comrades and colleagues of those still languishing in prisons. It was the Indian state, with its immense power and vast resources, that was scared of its writers, thinkers, scholars and activists. Its prisoners stood tall, laughed and sang in the face of unrelenting assaults.

When we took stock of the material we had lost, we understood that we had to go back to the families of political prisoners to be able to complete our project. This realisation came with the worry that we could cause further trouble as we would have to ask them one more time to relive and recount painful memories. While we wanted to tell this story, the last thing we wanted was to be a burden for any of the people for whom this book came into being in the first place. As we started hesitantly reaching out, we were once again overwhelmed – this time by the incredible amount of care, love and solidarity we were showered with. Everyone – irrespective of how challenging their own circumstances may have been – asked after Afreen and her well-being and offered to do anything in their capacity to help. Children, mothers and spouses went back to their drawers to look for the letters and the photos we needed. They once again opened their homes and their hearts and let us in, making us part of a phenomenal network of affection and solidarity.

Looking at India today, if there is a lesson to be learned from an authoritarian regime that presides over an 'undeclared emergency' and no longer makes any efforts at wearing the mask of democracy, it is that the seeds of hope and resistance cannot be killed – they may be invisible, even seem depleted for a time. Still, they will eventually find a way to return and bloom.

While the responsibility of mistakes and shortcomings is exclusively our own, this book has only been possible because of the love and trust of a community of people – inside and outside of prison – who believe in the power of nurturing these seeds of hope and resistance.

Acknowledgements

This book would not have been possible without the trust of the families of blood or election of the political prisoners. Our deepest gratitude for believing in this book goes to: Susan Abraham and Sagar Abraham Gonsalves; Sahba Husain; Shakira Begum and Syed Tafneef Hussain; Muzammil Imam; Rupali Jadhav; Najmuddin, Noor Jahan and Afzal Khan; Father Frazer Mascarenhas; P. Hemalatha and P. Pavana; Father Tony P.M.; Rinchin; Jenny Rowena; Nargis Saifi; Koel Sen; Ipsa Shaktasi; Bathool Shareef; Soni Sori; Prachi Teltumbde; Ramdas Unhale; Farzana Yasmeen; Father Joseph Xavier. Thank you to Sudha Bharadwaj, Devangana Kalita, Nodeep Kaur, Natasha Narwal, Varavara Rao, Asif Iqbal Tanha, Sharjeel Usmani, Safoora Zargar for your time, your words and all you do.

Ekta Mittal, Ram Bhat and all the team at maraa for sharing their work on the BK16 and being the initial spark of 'Profiles of Dissent.'

Pooja George and Vedika Inamdar for their commitment and for sharing with us the ups and downs at The Polis Project.

Tazeen Junaid for assisting in this book. Afreen Fatima for supporting in the research for the book and for her clarity.

International Solidarity for Academic Freedom in India and in particular Sruti Bala for their generosity, support and solidarity. Avinash Kumar for his selfless support and encouragement. Sarfaraz Sheikh for his support. Lotika Singha for the unconditional love she showed for the book.

Sanjay Kak, Nadeem Khan, Biju Mathew, Tamanna Pankaj and advocate Akash Sorde, Pandu Narote's lawyer, for their time and thoughts. Shaheen Abdulla, Sabah Gurmat, Md Meherbaan and Mohammad Sartaj Alam for helping with contacts.

A special thanks goes to Indian journalists who continue to report courageously from the ground. Through their work it was possible for us to corroborate, complement, expand and deepen our knowledge, research and archive.

Thank you Neda Tehrani, our wonderful editor at Pluto Press, who believed in this book from the inception and supported us through this journey.

Other people helped in many different ways but wish to remain anonymous for legal reasons or for safety: an individual thanks goes to each one of them.

We owe much to our families for putting up with daughters like us.

Finally, thanks to Meera and Emma for being the future.

Bibliography

Aafaq, Zafar, 'India police crack down on protests against Prophet remarks.' *Al Jazeera*, 11 June 2022. www.aljazeera.com/news/2022/6/11/india-two-killed-during-protests-over-prophet-muhammad-remarks (last accessed October 2022).

Ahmad, Irfan, 'Violence after violence: the politics of narratives over the Delhi pogrom.' *The Polis Project*, 28 March 2020. www.thepolisproject.com/read/violence-after-violence-the-politics-of-narratives-over-the-delhi-pogrom/ (last accessed May 2022).

Ajotikar, Rasika, 'Our song impure, our voice polluted': conversations with activist and musician Shital Sathe.' *Feminist Review*, 119, 2018: 154–62.

Akam, Shahrukh, 'In criminalising political action, judges are helping the state bring politics into India's Court.' *The Wire*, 29 October 2022. https://thewire.in/law/courts-these-days-unselfconsciously-criminalise-political-action (last accessed November 2022).

Ambedkar, Rama Teltumbde, 'Reflecting on the most poignant moments of last two years during Anand's incarceration.' *The Leaflet*, 14 April 2022. https://theleaflet.in/reflecting-on-the-most-poignant-moments-of-Last-two-years-during-anands-incarceration/ (last accessed May 2022).

Anonymous, 'Living in a time not mine: an anonymous letter from inside an Israeli prison.' *Skin Deep*, 8 August 2022. https://skindeepmag.com/articles onfineee-anonymous-letter-inside-israeli-prison-incarceration-administrative-detention (last accessed August 2022).

Ashraf, Ajaz, '"At times, without mamma, I feel desperate," says daughter of jailed lawyer Sudha Bharadwaj.' *Scroll.in*, 26 January 2019. https://scroll.in/article/910718/at-times-without-mamma-i-feel-desperate-says-jailed-activist-sudha-bharadwajs-daughter (last accessed August 2022).

——, 'My spirit has not been broken: activist Sudha Bharadwaj.' *News Click*, 27 January 2022. www.newsclick.in/my-spirit-has-not-been-broken-activist-sudha-bharadwaj (last accessed August 2022).

——, 'And she waits for Umar Khalid.' *Mid-day*, 4 April 2022. www.mid-day.com/news/opinion/article/and-she-waits-for-umar-khalid-23221299 (last accessed June 2022).

——, 'And she waits for Gautam Navlakha.' *Mid-day*, 9 May 2022. www.mid-day.com/news/opinion/article/and-she-waits-for-gautam-navlakha-23226310 (last accessed May 2022).

——, 'And he waits for Shoma Sen.' *Mid-day*, 16 May 2022. https://origin.mid-day.com/news/opinion/article/and-he-waits-for-shoma-sen-23227324 (last accessed June 2022).

——, 'And Ammi weeps for Sharjeel Imam.' *Mid-day*, 30 May 2022. www.mid-day. com/news/opinion/article/and-ammi-weeps-for-sharjeel-imam-23229396 (last accessed June 2022).

——, 'And Ma can't sing with Sagar.' *Mid-day*, 6 June 2022. www.mid-day.com/ news/opinion/article/and-ma-cant-sing-with-sagar-23230447 (last accessed June 2022).

——, 'And comrades admire Jyoti Jagtap.' *Mid-day*, 11 July 2022. www.mid-day. com/news/opinion/article/and-comrades-admire-jyoti-jagtap-23235308 (last accessed July 2022).

——, 'And wish a bride for Meeran Haider.' *Mid-day*, 8 August 2022. www.mid-day. com/news/opinion/article/and-wish-a-bride-for-meeran-haider-23239881 (last accessed August 2022).

Bentivogli, Agnese, 'Una via di mezzo tra esilio e prigionia: il confino, l'arma di repressione silenziosa del regime fascista.' *Parentesi Storiche*, 18 October 2018. https://parentesistoriche.altervista.org/confino-fascismo/ (last accessed January 2023).

Chakravarty, Ipsita, 'A chilling judgment sentences Delhi academician GN Saibaba to life in prison.' *Scroll.in*, 8 March 2017. https://scroll.in/article/831192/ the-daily-fix-a-chilling-judgment-sentences-delhi-academician-gn-saibaba-to-life-in-prison (last accessed November 2022).

Chowdhury, Sohini, 'Supreme Court stays release of Prof GN Saibaba & others in UAPA case, suspends Bombay HC's acquittal order.' *LiveLaw.in*, 15 October 2022. www.livelaw.in/top-stories/prof-gn-saibaba-delhi-uni-supreme-court-bombay-hc-acquittal-suspended-uapa-sanction-211735 (last accessed October 2022).

Coordination of Democratic Rights Organisations, Indian Association Peoples' Lawyers and Women Against Sexual Violence and State Repression, *Encountering Resistance: State Policy for Development in Gadchiroli*. *People's Union for Democratic Rights*, 2018.

Cover, Robert M., 'Foreword: nomos and narrative.' *Harvard Law Review*, 97, 1983. https://heinonline.org/hol-cgi-bin/get_pdf.cgi?handle=hein.journals/ hlr97&section=13 (last accessed October 2022).

——, 'Violence and the word.' *The Yale Law Journal*, 95, 1986: 1601–29.

——, *Narrative, violence, and the law: the essays of Robert Cover*. University of Michigan Press, 1992.

Dahat, Pavan, 'Govt. wanted to kill me: Saibaba.' *The Hindu*, 8 April 2016. www. thehindu.com/news/national/G.N.-Saibaba-says-government-wanted-to-kill-him/article60319957.ece (last accessed November 2022).

Daniyal, Shoaib, 'Saibaba conviction: how a draconian law has turned mere thought into crime.' *Scroll.in*, 9 March 2017. https://scroll.in/article/831282/ saibaba-conviction-how-the-uapa-introduced-the-concept-of-thoughtcrime-into-indian-legislation (last accessed November 2022).

Deb, Siddhartha, 'The unravelling of a conspiracy: were the 16 charged with plotting to kill India's prime minister framed?' *The Guardian*, 12 August 2021. www.theguardian.com/world/2021/aug/12/bhima-koregaon-case-india-conspiracy-modi (last accessed October 2022).

Democratic Decline, 'Sahba Husain on Gautam Navlakha.' www.youtube.com/ watch?v=2pB3wrndN-A (last accessed August 2022).

Dixit, Neha, 'The Prisoner's wife in a jailed republic.' *The Wire*, 6 August 2021. https://thewire.in/rights/the-prisoners-wife-in-a-jailed-republic (last accessed August 2022).

DNA Web Team, 'Timeline: from DU English professor to convicted Maoist, how the GN Saibaba case unfolded.' *DNA*, 7 March 2017. www.dnaindia.com/india/ report-timeline-from-du-english-professor-to-convicted-maoist-how-the-gn-saibaba-case-unfolded-2345329 (last accessed October 2022).

EKALAVYA, 'Political repression, political prisoners: fighting the class war in India.' *Crime and Social Justice*, 1974: 4–11.

Emerson, John, 'Being neutral is our biggest crime.' *Human Rights Watch*, 25 June 2015. www.hrw.org/report/2008/07/14/being-neutral-our-biggest-crime/ government-vigilante-and-naxalite-abuses-indias (last accessed November 2022).

Fatima, Heena, '"Cops pry kids' hands from their father's grasp": what families of "political prisoners" face.' *The Print*, 30 July 2022. https://theprint.in/features/ cops-pry-kids-hands-from-their-fathers-grasp-what-families-of-political-prisoners-face/1061169/ (last accessed August 2022).

Fernández, Adolfo Naya, *Operation 'Green Hunt' in India: Social Practices of the Genocidal Counter-insurgency strategy 'Hearts and Minds.'* Foreign languages Press, 2020.

Ferreira, Arun, *Colours of the Cage: A Prison Memoir*. Aleph Book Company, 2014.

Friedrich, Pieter, 'Cultural malware: the rise of India's RSS.' *The Polis Project*, 12 March 2020. www.thepolisproject.com/read/cultural-malware-the-rise-of-indias-rss/ (last accessed July 2022).

Gellately, Robert, 'The Gestapo and German society: political denunciation in the Gestapo case files.' *The Journal of Modern History*, 60 (4), 1988: 654–94.

George, Pooja and Vedika Inamdar, 'Mainstream news media and majoritarian state violence in India.' *The Polis Project*, 9 December 2021. www.thepolisproject. com/read/mainstream-news-media-and-majoritarian-state-violence-in-india/ (last accessed July 2022).

Giri, Saroj, 'The Bhima Koregaon arrests and the resistance in India.' *Monthly Review*, 12 November 2022. https://monthlyreview.org/2022/04/01/the-bhima-koregaon-arrests-and-the-resistance-in-india-2/ (last accessed November 2022).

Global Freedom of Expression Staff, 'Binayak Sen v. Chhatisgarh.' *Global Freedom of Expression*, 6 July 2021. globalfreedomofexpression.columbia.edu/cases/ binayak-sen-v-chhatisgarh/ (last accessed November 2022).

Gonsalves, Vernon, '"You are immortalised in our hearts": a cellmate's letter to Stan Swamy on his death anniversary.' *Scroll.in*, 5 July 2022. https://scroll.in/ article/1027594/you-are-immortalised-in-all-our-hearts-a-cellmates-letter-to-stan-swamy-on-his-death-anniversary (last accessed July 2022).

Gramsci, Antonio, *Quaderni dal carcere*. Einaudi, 2014 (originally published 1975).

Grey, Deborah, 'Death of a rationalist: Gauri Lankesh.' *CJP*, 13 May 2018. https://cjp.org.in/death-of-a-rationalist-gauri-lankesh/ (last accessed January 2023).

Gurlhosur, Geetanjali, 'Kabir Kala Manch: a history of revolutionary singing and state repression.' *Ritimo*, 7 April 2022. www.ritimo.org/Kabir-Kala-Manch-A-History-of-Revolutionary-Singing-and-State-Repression (last accessed November 2022).

Hakim, Sharmeen, 'Elgar Parishad case: Bombay High Court denies bail to Jyoti Jagtap.' *LiveLaw.in*, 17 October 2022. www.livelaw.in/news-updates/elgar-parishad-case-bombay-high-court-denies-bail-to-jyoti-jagtap-211829#:~:text=The%20Bombay%20High%20Court%20on,the%20banned%20CPI%20(Maoist) (last accessed November 2022).

Hansen, Thomas Blom, *The Saffron Wave: Democracy and Hindu Nationalism in Modern India*. Princeton University Press, 1999.

Honoring the life and legacy of Father Stan, H. R. 1219, 117th Cong. (2021), 5 July 2022. www.congress.gov/117/bills/hres1219/BILLS-117hres1219ih.xml (last accessed August 2022).

hooks, bell, *All about Love: New Visions*. Harper Perennial, 2001.

Human Rights Council Working Group on Arbitrary Detention, 'Opinions adopted by the Working Group on Arbitrary Detention at its ninety-second session, 15–19 November 2021.' *United Nations Human Rights Office of the High Commissioner*, 14 February 2022. www.ohchr.org/sites/default/files/2022-03/A-HRC-WGAD-2021-57-India-AEV.pdf (last accessed October 2022).

Human Rights Watch, 'Shoot the traitors.' *Human Rights Watch*, 16 June 2020. www.hrw.org/report/2020/04/09/shoot-traitors/discrimination-against-muslims-under-indias-new-citizenship-policy (last accessed November 2022).

Indie Journal, 'Exclusive: भीमा कोरेगाव खटल्यात कैद ज्येष्ठ वकील सुरेंद्र गडलगि यांचं तुरुंगातून पत्र.' *Indie Journal*, 8 April 2021. www.indiejournal.in/article/exclusive-surendra-gadling-writes-letter-from-prison-to-kanchan-nannaware (last accessed September 2022).

Irfan, Hanan and Mohd Kashif, 'The scapegoating of Sharjeel Imam.' *Maktoob Media*, 28 May 2022. https://maktoobmedia.com/2022/05/28/scapegoating-of-sharjeel-imam/ (last accessed August 2022).

InSAF India, 'Jailed to die? India's incarcerated human rights defenders and the Covid emergency.' 19 June 2021. www.youtube.com/watch?v=wBDloay253g (last accessed August 2022).

Jamshedpur Jesuits, 'I am not a silent spectator.' 3 August 2021. www.youtube.com/watch?v=ssS2PSQBpUo (last accessed August 2022).

Jeelani, Mehboob, 'The best way to stop me was to throw me in jail, says Saibaba.' *The Hindu*, 6 July 2015. www.thehindu.com/news/national/Professor-G.N.-Saibaba-The-best-way-to-stop-me-was-to-throw-me-in-jail/article60515789.ece (last accessed November 2022).

Jha, Satish, 'SC order on Zakia Jafri's appeal "illegal, Unconstitutional and Violates Every Tenet of law".' *CJP*, 8 July 2022. cjp.org.in/sc-order-on-zakia-jafris-appeal-illegal-unconstitutional-and-violates-every-tenet-of-law/ (last accessed November 2022).

Johnson, T.A., 'Explained: Dabholkar-Lankesh murders – what the investigations into violent right-wing activism show.' *The Indian Express*, 26 May 2019. https://indianexpress.com/article/explained/explained-dabholkar-lankesh-murders-investigations-right-wing-activismv-cbi-sit-pansare-kalburgi-5749338/ (last accessed January 2023).

Jones, Reece, 'Geopolitical boundary narratives, the global war on terror and border fencing in India.' *Transactions of the Institute of British Geographers*, 34, 2009: 290–304.

Kalhan, Anil, Gerald P. Conroy, Mamta Kaushal, Sam Scott Miller and Jed S. Rakoff, 'Colonial continuities: human rights, terrorism, and security laws in India.' *Columbia Journal of Asian Law*, 20(1), 2006.

Kalita, Devangana and Natasha Narwal, '"Love and rage": Natasha and Devangana's letters of hope and resistance from Tihar Jail 6.' *The Caravan*, 13 June 2021. https://caravanmagazine.in/crime/love-and-rage-natasha-narwal-devangana-kalita-letters-tihar-jail (last accessed May 2022).

Kannabiran, K.G., *The Wages of Impunity: Power, Justice and Human Rights*. Orient Blackswan, 2018.

Khalid, Umar, 'Umar Khalid on his two years in jail: "I feel pessimistic at times. and also lonely".' *The Wire*, 13 September 2022. https://thewire.in/rights/umar-khalid-on-his-two-years-in-jail-i-feel-pessimistic-at-times-and-also-lonely (last accessed September 2022).

Khan, Fatima, '"Atikur Rahman's left side paralysed": kin of activist arrested in Hathras case.' *The Quint*, 2 September 2022. www.thequint.com/news/india/atikur-rahman-heart-patient-paralysed-hathras (last accessed September 2022).

Kochhar, Rajan, 'Civil society heading to the danger of a new frontier; are we prepared?' *India Times*, 7 February 2022. https://government.economictimes.indiatimes.com/news/governance/opinion-civil-society-heading-to-the-danger-of-a-new-frontier-are-we-prepared/89403679 (last accessed January 2023).

Kolhatkar, Neeta, '"The State snatched away my time with my daughter".' *Rediff.com*, 4 February 2022. www.rediff.com/news/interview/sudha-bharadwaj-the-state-snatched-away-my-time-with-my-daughter/20220203.htm (last accessed August 2022).

Krishnankutty, Pia, 'Civil society is new frontier of war, can be subverted to harm nation, Ajit Doval says.' *The Print*, 13 November 2021. https://theprint.in/india/civil-society-is-new-frontier-of-war-can-be-subverted-to-harm-nation-ajit-doval-says/765748/ (last accessed January 2023).

Kumar, Akanksha, 'How a Malayala Manorama journalist's suspicions about Kappan figure in UP police chargesheet.' *Newslaundry*, 28 December 2021. www.newslaundry.com/2021/12/28/how-a-malayala-manorama-journalists-suspicions-about-kappan-figure-in-up-police-chargesheet (last accessed September 2022).

Lahiri, Banojyotsna, 'As my friend Umar spends another birthday in jail, our fight for freedom goes on.' *The Quint*, 13 September 2022. www.thequint.com/

voices/opinion/umar-khalid-jail-freedom-friendship (last accessed September 2022).

Levi, Carlo, *Cristo si è fermato a Eboli*. Einaudi, 2014 (originally published 1945).

Lines, Rick, 'The right to health of prisoners in international human rights law.' *International Journal of Prisoner Health*, 4 (1), March 2008: 3–53. https://doi.org/10.1080/17449200701862145 (last accessed September 2022).

Livelaw News Network, 'Delhi HC hearing in plea for probe into Delhi riots.' *LiveLaw.in*, 26 February 2020. www.livelaw.in/top-stories/live-updates-delhi-hc-hearing-in-plea-for-probe-into-delhi-riots-153160 (last accessed November 2022).

——, 'Bhima Koregaon case: Supreme Court extends interim protection of Varavara Rao; adjourns bail plea to July 19.' *LiveLaw.in*, 12 July 2022. www.livelaw.in/top-stories/bhima-koregaon-case-supreme-court-extends-interim-protection-of-varavara-rao-adjourns-bail-plea-to-july-19-203516 (last accessed July 2022).

——, 'Siddique Kappan has deep links with terror funding organizations like PFI: UP govt tells Supreme Court.' *LiveLaw.in*, 6 September 2022. www.livelaw.in/top-stories/siddique-kappan-has-deep-links-with-terror-funding-organizations-like-pfiup-govt-tells-supreme-court-208530 (last accessed September 2022).

Lokaneeta, Jinee, *The Truth Machines: Policing, Violence, and Scientific Interrogations in India*. University of Michigan Press, 2020.

Lokur, Madan B., A.P. Shah, R.S. Sodhi, Anjana Prakash, G.K. Pillai, *Uncertain Justice: A Citizens Committee Report on the North East Delhi Violence 2020*. Constitutional Conduct Group, 7 October 2022. https://indianculturalforum.in/2022/10/07/uncertain-justice-a-citizens-committee-report-on-the-north-east-delhi-violence-2020/ (last accessed November 2022).

Longerich, Peter, *Goebbels: A Biography*. Random House, 2015.

Louis, Prakash, *Fr. Stan Swamy: A Maoist or a Martyr?* South Vision Books, 2022.

Mahadevan, Sneha, 'Fight for freedom.' *The Indian Express*, 16 April 2010. https://indianexpress.com/article/news-archive/web/fight-for-freedom/ (last accessed August 2022).

Maktoob Staff, '"Siddique Kappan is chained to cot like an animal in hospital", lawyer in an urgent letter to CJI.' *Maktoob Media*, 24 April 2021. https://maktoobmedia.com/2021/04/24/siddique-kappan-is-chained-to-cot-like-an-animal-in-hospital-lawyer-in-an-urgent-letter-to-cji/ (last accessed September 2022).

——, 'Bombay HC rejects Hany Babu's bail plea, says "prime facie conspired".' *Maktoob Media*, 19 September 2022. https://maktoobmedia.com/2022/09/19/bombay-hc-rejects-hany-babus-bail-plea-says-prime-facie-conspired/ (last accessed September 2022).

Mamet, Elliot, 'This unfortunate development': incarceration and democracy in W. E. B. Du Bois.' *Political Theory*. https://doi.org/10.1177/00905917221104503 (last accessed August 2022).

Mandal, Nilkantha, Sandeep Pandey and Kushagra Kumar, 'The man who used to get people acquitted in false cases has been implicated in one himself.'

Mainstream, LIX (2), 26 December 2020. www.mainstreamweekly.net/article10257.html (last accessed October 2022).

Mandela, Ndileka, 'Ndileka Mandela: without intervention, India risks becoming an apartheid state.' *Toronto Star*, 22 July 2022. www.thestar.com/opinion/contributors/2022/07/22/ndileka-mandela-without-intervention-india-risks-becoming-an-apartheid-state.html (last accessed August 2022).

maraa, *Read Aloud. Ideas Can Never Be Arrested.* Self-published, 2019.

Masih, Niha, 'Hackers planted evidence on computer of jailed Indian priest, report says.' *The Washington Post*, 13 December 2022. www.washingtonpost.com/world/2022/12/13/stan-swamy-hacked-bhima-koregaon/ (last accessed January 2023).

Masih, Niha and Joanna Slater, 'They were accused of plotting to overthrow the Modi government. The evidence was planted, a new report says.' *The Washington Post*, 12 November 2022. www.washingtonpost.com/world/asia_pacific/india-bhima-koregaon-activists-jailed/2021/02/10/8087f172-61e0-11eb-a177-7765f29a9524_story.html (last accessed November 2022).

Menon, Aditya and Aishwarya Iyer, '"Kaat do" said Ragini Tiwari, "eyewitness" saw her firing bullets.' *The Quint*, 30 June 2020. www.thequint.com/news/politics/delhi-violence-probe-riots-ragni-tiwari-hindutva-bjp-muslims (last accessed November 2022).

Menon, Shruti and Sreenivasan Jain, 'Videos of Bhima-Koregaon speeches offer a rebuttal to "Maoist" Claim.' *NDTV*, 4 September 2018. www.ndtv.com/india-news/videos-of-bhima-koregaon-speeches-at-elgar-parishad-offer-a-rebuttal-to-maoist-claim-1911415 (last accessed November 2022).

Mittal, Sumedha and Amir Malik, 'Three eyewitnesses accuse Delhi police official of murder during Delhi violence.' *The Caravan*, 12 February 2021. https://caravanmagazine.in/crime/three-eyewitnesses-accuse-delhi-police-official-murder-during-delhi-violence (last accessed November 2022).

Modak, Sadaf, 'Days after Vernon Gonsalves contracts dengue, Gautam Navlakha approaches court again seeking mosquito net.' *The Indian Express*, 13 September 2022. https://indianexpress.com/article/cities/mumbai/days-after-gonsalves-contracts-dengue-navlakha-approaches-court-again-seeking-mosquito-net-8149196/ (last accessed September 2022).

Narrain, Arvind, *India's Undeclared Emergency: Constitutionalism and the Politics of Resistance.* Context, 2022.

Newsclick Staff, 'G.N. Saibaba being persecuted for his ideas? by Gautam Navlakha.' *NewsClick*, 14 March 2017. www.youtube.com/watch?v=YcKYHNlaedk&t=107s (last accessed November 2022).

Newslaundry Staff, 'Siddique Kappan chargesheet.' *Newslaundry*, 9 September 2022. www.newslaundry.com/media/the-siddique-kappan-chargesheet (last accessed September 2022).

Nileena, M.S., 'Bhima Koregaon inmates can barely communicate, worried about their health: families'. *The Caravan*, 12 July 2020. https://caravanmagazine.in/politics/bhima-koregaon-inmates-can-barely-communicate-worried-about-their-health-families (last accessed May 2022).

Ojha, Srishti, 'There's no urgency, heavens don't fall:' Supreme Court on Request for fixed date for plea to prevent attacks against Christians.' *LiveLaw.in*, 26 April 2022. www.livelaw.in/top-stories/supreme-court-plea-to-prevent-attacks-against-christians-197601 (last accessed October 2022).

Outlook Web Desk, 'A midnight meeting on Feb 27 and a murdered minister.' *Outlook India*, 12 November 2007. www.outlookindia.com/magazine/story/a-midnight-meeting-on-feb-27-and-a-murdered-minister/235982 (last accessed January 2023).

Padel, Felix and Samarendra Das, *Anthropology of a Genocide: Tribal Movements in Central India against Over-industralisation.* SAAG, 2006.

Pal, Sumedha, 'Prayagraj protests: "being framed", say anti-CAA protesters as police name them "key conspirators".' *The Wire*, 11 June 2022. https://thewire.in/rights/prayagraj-protests-anti-caa-uttar-pradesh-police (last accessed October 2022).

Parmar, Tekendra, 'The persecution of GN Saibaba and India's "annihilation" of the resistance.' *The Nation*, 3 May 2018. www.thenation.com/article/archive/the-persecution-of-gn-saibaba-and-indias-annihilation-of-the-resistance/ (last accessed November 2022).

Pasha, Seemi, 'The Delhi violence FIRs are like blank cheques, to be encashed by the police any time.' *The Wire*, 30 April 2020. thewire.in/communalism/the-delhi-violence-firs-are-like-blank-cheques-to-be-encashed-by-the-police-any-time (last accessed November 2022).

Pelly, Grace, 'State terrorism: torture, extra-judicial killings, and forced disappearances in India: report of the Independent People's Tribunal.' *Socio Legal Information Centre*, 9–10 February 2008.

People's Union for Civil Liberties, 'Analysis of the case against Dr. Binayak Sen.' *PUCL*, 21 July 2007. https://web.archive.org/web/20110921154633/www.pucl.org/Topics/Human-rights/2007/sen-case-analysis.html (last accessed November 2022).

People's Union for Democratic Rights, *Banned and Damned. SIMI's Saga with UAPA Tribunals.* PUDR, June 2015. www.pudr.org/banned-and-damned-simis-saga-uapa-tribunals (last accessed August 2022).

Poddar, Umang, 'Punished without trial: how India's political prisoners are being denied basic rights in jail.' *Scroll.in*, 9 August 2022. https://scroll.in/article/1029553/punished-without-trial-how-indias-political-prisoners-are-being-denied-basic-rights-in-jail (last accessed August 2022).

Prabhu, Vidya, 'Fight for freedom.' *The Indian Express*, 6 November 2011. https://indianexpress.com/article/news-archive/web/fight-for-freedom-2/ (last accessed August 2022).

Press Statement from teachers of Delhi University, 'Statements against police raid at GN Saibaba's house.' *Sanhati*, 13 September 2013. http://sanhati.com/articles/7991/ (last accessed November 2022).

Press Trust of India, 'Mere membership of banned organisation not a crime: Supreme Court.' *The Hindu*, 4 February 2011. www.thehindu.com/news/national/Mere-membership-of-banned-organisation-not-a-crime-Supreme-Court/article15127515.ece (last accessed November 2022).

——, 'Probe agency opposes activist Stan Swamy's bail plea, calls him Maoist.' *NDTV*, 17 June 2021. www.ndtv.com/india-news/probe-agency-nia-opposes-activist-stan-swamys-bail-plea-in-elgar-parishad-case-call-him-maoist-2466435 (last accessed January 2023).

——, 'Delhi riots: HC asks police to respond to bail plea of student activist in larger conspiracy case.' *The Indian Express*, 11 May 2022. indianexpress.com/article/cities/delhi/delhi-northeast-riots-2020-high-court-bail-pleaogulfisha-fatima-7910971/ (last accessed November 2022).

——, 'Jailed professor GN Saibaba threatens indefinite strike unless CCTV removed from cell.' *Firstpost*, 15 May 2022. www.firstpost.com/india/jailed-professor-gn-saibaba-threatens-indefinite-strike-unless-cctv-removed-from-cell-10677351.html (last accessed June 2022).

Priya, Ilika, 'शहीद क्रांतिकारी जतिन दास की शहादत के मौके पर जेल की समस्याओं को लेकर पत्रकार रूपेश अनशन पर.' *Janchowk*, 13 September 2022. https://janchowk.com/statewise/journalist-rupesh-sat-on-hunger-strike/ (last accessed September 2022).

Quill Foundation, 'Brutalizing innocence – testimonies of torture and police violence against minors by UP Police.' *The Polis Project*, 15 March 2020. www.thepolisproject.com/read/brutalising-innocence-testimonies-of-torture-and-police-violence-against-minors-by-up-police/ (last accessed June 2022).

Rajagopal, Krishnadas, 'Supreme Court changes stand; now mere membership of a banned outfit is a crime under UAPA.' The Hindu, 24 March 2023. https://www.thehindu.com/news/national/sc-clarifies-mere-membership-of-banned-organisation-will-make-person-criminally-liable-under-uapa/article66656190.ece (last accessed March 2023).

Rao, Anupama, 'Violence and humanity: or, vulnerability as political subjectivity.' *Social Research: An International Quarterly*, 78 (4), 2011: 607–32.

——, 'Stigma and labour: remembering Dalit Marxism.' *Seminar*, Issue 633, May 2012. www.india-seminar.com/2012/633/633_anupama_rao.htm (last accessed January 2023).

Rao, Varavara, *Captive Imagination: Letters from Prison*. Viking, 2010.

Rautray, Samanwaya, 'Greater scrutiny of RAW & IB will risk own existence: Supreme Court.' *The Economic Times*, 14 July 2018. https://economictimes.indiatimes.com/news/defence/greater-scrutiny-of-raw-ib-will-risk-own-existence-supreme-court/articleshow/51114192.cms?from=mdr (last accessed January 2023).

Recchia, Francesca and Suchitra Vijayan, 'In India, social media is a lifeline. It's being silenced.' *The Washington Post*, 6 May 2021. www.washingtonpost.com/opinions/2021/05/06/india-social-media-covid-19/ (last accessed October 2022).

——, 'Who do we call when the Police murders? Fear grows as the Indian Muslim community is under constant attack.' *The Polis Project*, 21 June 2022. www.thepolisproject.com/read/who-do-we-call-when-the-police-murders-fear-grows-as-the-indian-muslim-community-is-under-constant-attack/ (last accessed October 2022).

Roy, Arundhati, *Azadi: Freedom. Fascism. Fiction*. Penguin, 2020.

Roy Chowdhury, Shreya, 'G N Saibaba: the revolutionary in Delhi University.' *The Times of India*, 26 September 2013. https://timesofindia.indiatimes.com/city/delhi/g-n-saibaba-the-revolutionary-in-delhi-university/articleshow/23104776.cms (last accessed November 2022).

SabrangIndia, 'The death of Fr. Stan Swamy was finalised the day he was arrested: Senior Advocate Mihir Desai.' *SabrangIndia*, 26 December 2022. https://sabrangindia.in/article/death-fr-stan-swamy-was-finalised-day-he-was-arrested-senior-advocate-mihir-desai (last accessed January 2023).

Sagar, 'Hindu supremacist mobs orchestrate violence against Muslims where BJP won in Delhi elections.' *The Caravan*, 25 February 2020. https://caravanmagazine.in/religion/delhi-violence-north-east-maujpur-jaffrabad-babarpur-muslims-hindu (last accessed November 2022).

——, 'Main Yashwant Shinde Bol Raha Hoon.' *The Caravan*, 30 September 2022. https://caravanmagazine.in/crime/rss-worker-yashwant-shinde-interview-hindu-terrorism-rss-vhp-mohan-bhagwat (last accessed October 2022).

Sanhati Collective, 'List of victims of Operation Green Hunt in Chhattisgarh since August 2009.' *Sanhati*, 13 June 2011. http://sanhati.com/excerpted/3665 (last accessed November 2022).

Saran, Tishya, 'Umar Khalid's speech hateful & inciteful': Delhi High Court during oral exchange in plea challenging refusal of bail.' *LawBeat*, 22 April 2022. https://lawbeat.in/news-updates/umar-khalids-speech-hateful-inciteful-delhi-high-court-during-oral-exchange-plea (last accessed January 2023).

Sarothi Ray, Partho, 'Political Prisoners Unite the British Raj and "New India".' *The Wire*, 13 September 2022. https://thewire.in/rights/political-prisoners-unite-the-british-raj-and-new-india (last accessed October 2022).

Schwartzapfel, Beth, 'Prison money diaries: what people really make (and spend) behind bars.' *The Marshall Project*, 4 August 2022. www.themarshallproject.org/2022/08/04/prison-money-diaries-what-people-really-make-and-spend-behind-bars?utm_campaign=mb&utm_medium=newsletter&utm_source=morning_brew (last accessed August 2022).

Scroll Staff, 'Shaheen Bagh protestors will "rape your sisters and daughters", says BJP MP on women-led protest.' *Scroll.in*, 20 January 2020. https://scroll.in/latest/951341/shaheen-bagh-protestors-will-enter-houses-rape-sisters-and-daughters-claims-bjp-mp-parvesh-verma (last accessed November 2022).

——, 'Bombay HC judge withdraws comments praising Stan Swamy after NIA raises objection.' *Scroll.in*, 23 July 2021. https://scroll.in/latest/1000945/bombay-hc-judge-withdraws-comments-praising-stan-swamy-after-nia-raises-objection (last accessed August 2022).

——, 'Bhima Koregaon case: NIA court begins hearing discharge applications of accused persons.' *Scroll.in*, 28 September 2022. https://scroll.in/latest/1033878/bhima-koregaon-case-trial-process-begins-over-four-years-after-case-was-registered (last accessed September 2022).

——, 'Gautam Navlakha to be shifted to hospital, Supreme Court orders jail authorities.' *Scroll.in*, 29 September 2022. https://scroll.in/latest/1033947/gautam-navlakha-to-be-released-from-jail-put-under-house-arrest-orders-supreme-court (last accessed October 2022).

Sen, Arijit, 'Manipur's long wait for justice: remembering 1,528 cases and the murder of Thangjam Manorama.' *The Polis Project*, 22 November 2021. www.thepolisproject.com/read/manipurs-long-wait-for-justice-remembering-1528-cases-and-the-murder-of-thangjam-manorama/ (last accessed November 2022).

Sen, Shoma, 'The sad saga of Kanchan Nannaware who died waiting for justice.' *The Leaflet*, 9 March 2021. https://theleaflet.in/the-sad-saga-of-kanchan-nannaware-who-died-waiting-for-justice/ (last accessed October 2022).

Setalvad, Teesta in conversation with V.N. Rai, 'No riot can last for more than 24 hours unless the state wants it to continue.' *SabrangIndia*, February 1995. www.sabrangindia.in/interview/no-riot-can-last-more-24-hours-unless-state-wants-it-continue (last accessed November 2022).

Sethi, Aman, 'Green Hunt: the anatomy of an operation.' *The Hindu*, 6 February 2010. www.thehindu.com/opinion/op-ed/Green-Hunt-the-anatomy-of-an-operation/article16812797.ece (last accessed November 2022).

Shantha, Sukanya, 'Gadchiroli's 300 Gram Sabhas Pass Resolution in support of activist Mahesh Raut.' *The Wire*, 10 October 2018. https://thewire.in/rights/mahesh-raut-forest-rights-bhima-koregon (last accessed November 2022).

——, 'A reporter saw the Bhima Koregaon violence coming. Now, he fears for his life.' *The Wire*, 18 September 2020. https://thewire.in/caste/a-reporter-saw-the-bhima-koregaon-violence-coming-now-he-fears-for-his-life (last accessed November 2022).

——, 'Case against Hindutva leaders ignored, no justice in sight for Bhima Koregaon violence victims.' *The Wire*, 26 September 2020. https://thewire.in/caste/bhima-koregaon-violence-hindutva-leaders-case (last accessed November 2022).

——, 'NIA cites Kabir Kala Manch's Songs that parody Modi, BJP to justify arrest of singers.' *The Wire*, 14 December 2020. https://thewire.in/rights/nia-kabir-kala-mach-song-parody-modi-bjp-sagar-gorkhe-ramesh-gaichor-arrest (last accessed September 2022).

——, 'Awaiting trial for six years, UAPA prisoner dies while in custody.' *The Wire*, 25 January 2021. https://thewire.in/rights/uapa-undertrial-prisoner-death-custody (last accessed September 2022).

——, 'Bhima Koregaon violence: four different theories, but no justice in sight.' *The Wire*, 1 January 2022. https://thewire.in/rights/bhima-koregaon-violence-four-different-theories-but-no-justice-in-sight (last accessed September 2022).

——, 'Elgar Parishad case: Vernon Gonsalves is latest victim of prison staff's medical neglect.' *The Wire*, 8 September 2022. https://thewire.in/rights/elgar-parishad-case-vernon-gonsalves-latest-victim-medical-neglect (last accessed September 2022).

——, 'Top investigating officer admits elgar parishad event "had no role" in Bhima Koregaon violence.' *The Wire*, 27 December 2022. https://thewire.in/government/elgar-parishad-bhima-koregaon-connection (last accessed January 2023).

Sharma, Betwa, 'Talkative, evolving & never missing a "mulakat": Umar Khalid after 2 years in prison.' *Article14*, 13 September 2022. https://article-14.com/

post/talkative-evolving-never-missing-a-mulakat-umar-khalid-after-2-years-in-prison--631fff43a4297 (last accessed September 2022).

Sharma, Jeevan Prakash, 'Delhi riots 2020: here's why FIR No. 59 is so crucial to the case.' *Outlook*, 17 September 2020. www.outlookindia.com/website/story/india-news-delhi-riots-2020-heres-why-fir-no-59-is-so-crucial-to-the-case/360456/ (last accessed September 2022).

Shroff, Kaushal, 'Delhi violence: cops shouted "Jai Shri Ram" with armed Hindu mob, charged at Muslims.' *The Caravan*, 25 February 2020. https://caravanmagazine.in/conflict/delhi-violence-cops-shouted-jai-shri-ram-with-armed-hindu-mob-charged-at-muslims (last accessed November 2022).

Singh, Sonam, *Forbidden Notes | Documentary film about arrests of Kabir Kala Manch Members*, 2016. www.youtube.com/watch?v=gMYZhjGgLIQ (last accessed November 2022).

Singh Sengar, Mukesh, 'Cops got 7,500 calls for help on day 3 of Delhi violence: sources.' *NDTV*, 28 February 2020. www.ndtv.com/india-news/cops-got-7-500-calls-for-help-on-day-3-of-delhi-violence-sources-2187030 (last accessed January 2023).

Solzhenitsyn, Aleksandr, *The Gulag Archipelago 1918–56. An Experiment in Literary Investigation*. HarperCollins, 2007 (originally published 1900).

Suresh, V., S.B. Madhura and Lekshmi Sujatha, 'UAPA: criminalising dissent and state terror.' *PUCL*, 28 September 2022. www.pucl.org/reports/uapa-criminalising-dissent-and-state-terror (last accessed November 2022).

Sushmita, 'Hostile state machinery targets Dalits in Maharashtra.' *CJP*, 20 January 2018. cjp.org.in/hostile-state-machinery-targets-dalits-in-maharashtra/ (last accessed November 2022).

Swamy, Stan, *I Am Not a Silent Spectator*. Indian Social Institute, 2021.

Tandon, Deepika, 'Biting satire: when a mosquito net in jail is called a "security risk".' *The Quint*, 3 June 2022. www.thequint.com/neon/satire/biting-satire-mosquito-nets-called-security-risks-prison-bhima-koregaon (last accessed June 2022).

Teltumbde, Anand, 'How the state treats friends and foes of the oppressed.' *Economic and Political Weekly*, 44 (25), 20 June 2009. www.epw.in/journal/2009/25/commentary/how-state-treats-friends-and-foes-oppressed.html (last accessed November 2022).

——, 'Labelling Dalits and Adivasis as Maoists is an old state strategy for crushing dissent and criticism'. Excerpt from *Republic of Caste*, Scroll.in, 7 June 2018. https://scroll.in/article/881626/labelling-dalits-and-adivasis-as-maoists-is-an-old-state-strategy-for-crushing-dissent-and-criticism (last accessed November 2022).

Thakor, Harsh, 'Pandu Narote's death is a perfect illustration of neo-fascist murder by the state.' *Countercurrents*, 27 August 2022. https://countercurrents.org/2022/08/pandu-narotes-death-is-a-perfect-illustration-of-neo-fascist-murder-by-the-state/ (last accessed November 2022).

Thapar, Romila, *Voices of Dissent: An Essay*. Seagull Books, 2020.

Romila Thapar v. *Union of India* on 28 September 2018. https://indiankanoon.org/doc/52834611/ (last accessed October 2022).

Thapliyal, Nupur, '[Anti-CAA protests] trial pending in over 50% cases, probe incomplete in most FIRs: Delhi Police to HC.' *LiveLaw.in*, 21 September 2022. www.livelaw.in/news-updates/anti-caa-protests-trial-pending-public-private-properties-delhi-police-hc-209839 (last accessed September 2022).

——, 'Delhi riots: Delhi High Court's 10 reasons for denying bail to Umar Khalid in UAPA case.' *LiveLaw.in*, 18 October 2022. www.livelaw.in/news-updates/10-reasons-delhi-high-court-bail-umar-khalid-uapa-case-211973 (last accessed October 2022).

The News Beak, 'Roster Documentary: संघर्ष का एक किस्सा जो इतिहास में दर्ज हो गया। रोस्टर आंदोलन की पूरी कहानी.' www.youtube.com/watch?v=WreZf3LrgPI&t=11s (last accessed August 2022).

The Polis Project, 'Disproportionate and illegitimate state violence: a report on the police violence in Uttar Pradesh against anti-CAA protestors.' *The Polis Project*, 23 January 2020. www.thepolisproject.com/read/disproportionate-and-illegitimate-state-violence-a-report-on-the-police-violence-in-uttar-pradesh-against-anti-caa-protestors/ (last accessed September 2022).

——, 'The high cost of targeted violence in Northeast Delhi: a list of the deceased.' *The Polis Project*, 2 March 2020. www.thepolisproject.com/read/the-high-cost-of-targeted-violence-in-northeast-delhi-a-list-of-the-deceased/ (last accessed January 2023).

——, 'Manufacturing evidence: how the police are framing and arresting constitutional rights defenders in India.' *The Polis Project*, 13 August 2020. https://docs.google.com/viewerng/viewer?url=www.thepolisproject.com/wp-content/uploads/2020/08/Manufacturing-Evidence-1.pdf&hl=en (last accessed October 2022).

The Times of India, 'How Stan Swamy's long struggle for bail ended in tragedy', *The Times of India*, 5 July 2021. https://timesofindia.indiatimes.com/india/were-shocked-how-stan-swamys-long-struggle-for-bail-ended-in-tragedy/articleshow/84149059.cms (last accessed January 2023).

The Wire Staff, 'PM's rural development fellows come out in support of Mahesh Raut.' *The Wire*, 9 June 2018. https://thewire.in/rights/pms-rural-development-fellows-come-out-in-support-of-mahesh-raut (last accessed November 2022).

——, 'IPS officer who questioned Modi's role in Gujarat riots gets life in 30-year-old case.' *The Wire*, 20 June 2019. https://thewire.in/law/ips-officer-sanjiv-bhatt-custodial-death-narendra-modi-gujarat-riots (last accessed January 2023).

——, 'Citing instance of "witness" coercion, Umar Khalid accuses police of framing him in riots case.' *The Wire*, 2 September 2020. thewire.in/rights/citing-instance-of-witness-coercion-umar-khalid-accuses-police-of-framing-him-in-riots-case (last accessed November 2022).

——, 'Delhi riots conspiracy case "cooked up", was "framed by media": Umar Khalid.' *The Wire*, 23 August 2021. https://thewire.in/law/delhi-riots-conspiracy-case-cooked-up-framed-by-media-umar-khalid (last accessed January 2023).

——, 'Uttarakhand: activist Prashant Rahi acquitted in 2007 Maoist case.' *The Wire*, 14 January 2022. https://m.thewire.in/article/law/prashant-rahi-activist-acquitted-2007-uttarakhand-maoist-case/amp (last accessed August 2022).

Thiong'o, Ngũgĩ wa, *Detained: A Writer's Prison Diary*. Heinemann, 1981.

TNM Staff, '"My father's freedom has been broken": Siddique Kappan's daughter in I-Day speech.' *The News Minute*, 15 August 2022. www.thenewsminute. com/article/my-father-s-freedom-has-been-broken-siddique-kappans-daughter-i-day-speech-166862 (last accessed August 2022).

Usmani, Sharjeel, 'Let me be heard as a mere Muslim youth: Sharjeel Usmani's speech at Elgar Parishad.' *The Polis Project*, 4 February 2020. www. thepolisproject.com/read/let-me-be-heard-as-a-mere-muslim-youth-sharjeel-usmanis-speech-at-elgar-parishad/ (last accessed August 2022).

Various Authors, *Lettere di antifascisti dal carcere e dal confino*. Editori Riuniti, 1962–63.

Venkatesan, J., 'Binayak Sen gets bail in Supreme Court.' *The Hindu*, 15 April 2011. www.thehindu.com/news/national/Binayak-Sen-gets-bail-in-Supreme-Court/article14685491.ece (last accessed November 2022).

Venkatesan, V., 'A judicial stricture.' *Frontline Magazine*, 6 May 2004. https:// frontline.thehindu.com/other/article30222295.ece (last accessed November 2022).

Venugopal, N., *The Making of Varavara Rao*. Self-published, 2020.

Vijayan, Suchitra, *Midnight's Borders: A People's History of Modern India*. Melville House, 2021.

——, 'Authoritarianism and lies: how the Modi regime survives on the constant reinforcement of a fictional reality.' *The Polis Project*, 10 August 2021. www. thepolisproject.com/read/authoritarianism-and-lies-how-the-modi-regime-survives-on-the-constant-reinforcement-of-a-fictional-reality/ (last accessed May 2022).

Vijayan, Suchitra and Francesca Recchia, 'Modi's India is "one of the most dangerous countries for journalists".' *The Nation*, 8 November 2021. www. thenation.com/article/world/india-violence-journalists/ (last accessed October 2022).

Vincent, Pheroze L., 'Recounting the ordeal of famed undertrials inside Taloja prison.' *The Telegraph*, 14 April 2022. www.telegraphindia.com/india/recounting-the-ordeal-of-famed-undertrials-inside-taloja-prison/cid/1860581 (last accessed May 2022).

Wadekar, Disha, 'Understanding civil liberties from an Ambedkarite perspective.' *The Leaflet*, 14 April 2022. https://theleaflet.in/understanding-civil-liberties-from-an-ambedkarite-perspective/ (last accessed March 2023).

Watch The State, 'One year of farmers' protest: June 2020 to June 2021.' *The Polis Project*, 2 July 2021. www.thepolisproject.com/research/one-year-of-farmers-protests-in-india-june-2020-to-june-2021/ (last accessed June 2022).

Youth for Human Rights Documentation, 'An account of fear and impunity – a preliminary fact finding report on communally-targeted violence in NE Delhi, February 2020.' *The Polis Project*, 8 March 2020. www.thepolisproject.com/read/an-account-of-fear-impunity-a-preliminary-fact-finding-report-on-communally-targeted-violence-in-ne-delhi-february-2020/ (last accessed June 2022).

Zorey, Prasanna D., 'Dalit poet commits suicide in protest.' *Rediff*, date not listed. www.rediff.com/news/jul/16dalit1.htm (last accessed November 2022).